Object-Oriented
Databases

Other McGraw-Hill Books of Interest

*To order or receive additional information on these or any other
McGraw-Hill titles, please call 1-800-822-8158 in the United States. In
other countries, contact your local McGraw-Hill representative.*

BC14BCZ

Object-Oriented Databases

Technology, Applications, and Products

Bindu R. Rao

McGraw-Hill, Inc.

New York   San Francisco   Washington, D.C.   Auckland   Bogotá
Caracas   Lisbon   London   Madrid   Mexico City   Milan
Montreal   New Delhi   San Juan   Singapore
Sydney   Tokyo   Toronto

OBJECT-ORIENTED DATABASES
Technology, Applications, and Products
International Editions 1995

Exclusive rights by McGraw-Hill Book Co. – Singapore for manufacture and export. This book cannot be re-exported from the country to which it is consigned by McGraw-Hill.

1 2 3 4 5 6 7 8 9 0 CWP UPE 9 8 7 6 5

The sponsoring editor for this book was Marjorie Spencer, the editing supervisor was Jim Halston, and the production supervisor was Suzanne W. Babeuf. It was set in Century Schoolbook by McGraw-Hill's Professional Book group composition unit.

Library of Congress Cataloging-in-Publication Data

Rao, Bindu Rama.
    Object-oriented databases : technology, applications, and products / Bindu R. Rao.
        p.   cm.
    Includes index.
    ISBN 0-07-051279-5
    1. Object-oriented databases.   I. Title.
QA76.9.D3R267   1994
005.75–dc20   94-3115
                                                                CIP

When ordering this title, use ISBN 0-07-113642-8

Printed in Singapore

To Madhavi, Mukta, and Ravi

Contents

Preface

The ubiquitous use of databases should come as no surprise to any software developer. Almost every application that is written can, or does, employ some form of data storage facility. Databases are available on every hardware and software platform. In the last three decades, database technology has evolved from simple file manipulation systems to complex, yet versatile, information repositories. A survey through the literature shows the emergence of the object-oriented database technology as a solution to the problem of storing and retrieving complex data, typically n-dimensional data.

The database world is at the crossroads of technology. While the relational view of data has gained much credibility and a significant segment of the database market, its limitations have been exposed over and over again. While it is too early to declare the demise of relational technology, object-oriented database management systems (OODBMS) are gaining ground in the industry. Will the industry ever say: "Out with the old, in with the new?" It is amazing to find the whole spectrum of database technology in any given industry. There are several large corporations that often experiment with the leading edge of database technology while employing technology three generations behind the leading edge for their daily operations.

Migrating from an older technology to one that is new is often an uncertain and traumatic experience to all concerned. This is the case with the companies that have hitched their wagon to the OOT horse. There are no how-to books for these uncharted waters. Making the right decisions in choosing technology often seems like a black art and it takes much wizardry.

About This Book

This book has been designed to provide the reader with an introduction to the exciting world of object-oriented database management systems. The book emphasizes the object-oriented database (OODB) issues that make them so versatile and easy to use. The emphasis is on the how and why of OODBMS. The book begins with a brief introduction to the foundations of the object-oriented programming paradigm. Chapter 1 serves as a crash course in OOP. Chapter 2 is designed to provide a brief survey of object-oriented analysis (OOA) and design (OOD) methodologies. It is very important to provide reasons for employing newer technology, and Chapter 3 addresses this issue. Chapter 4 discusses what constitutes an OODBMS. Chapter 5 provides a detailed description of all OODBMS features.

Chapter 6 highlights the concepts of persistence and Chapter 7 explores object identity, and provides a good analysis of related issues. Chapter 8 gives a brief survey of OODB architectures. Chapters 9, 10, and 11 cover the commercial OODBMSs ObjectStore, Objectivity/DB, and Versant, respectively. Chapters 12 and 13 cover the issues related to the evaluation of OODBMS. These two are perhaps the two most useful chapters in the book for software developers interested in exploring OODBMS or migrating to OODBMS from the relational world.

Chapter 14 provides a detailed description of OMG's OMA architecture and focuses on CORBA and related issues. Chapter 15 provides a brief introduction to GemStone, Iris, and UniSQL OODBMSs. Chapter 16 covers some of the current research being done in the field. It also focuses on the next generation of DBMSs.

The book focuses on all the various OODBMS issues and on OODBMS products. I would like to ask my readers to use this book while embarking on a new project that plans to employ OODBMS for object storage and retrieval.

This book also offers a detailed introduction to the programming side of OODBMS applications. It helps to have a good background in object-oriented programming to get the maximum out of this book. It assumes a good background in the C++ programming language on the part of the audience.

This book is aimed at two specific audiences: professional software developers who have a good understanding of the software development process and who need to learn the new OODBMS technology, and college students taking a course on object-oriented databases. A strong background in relational databases and the C++ language programming would be a prerequisite for the reader.

For developers who are trying to migrate from traditional database environments to object-oriented database environments, this book can provide a strong theoretical introduction to the object-oriented database concepts as well as a fairly fast-paced introduction to OODBMS products in the market.

An extensive bibliography is provided at the end of each chapter to aid in further research.

Bindu Rama Rao

Acknowledgments

I am grateful to McGraw-Hill for providing me with the opportunity to write my second book.

There never seems to be enough time to finish a book. It is very hard to juggle all the activities of a modern-day working person and still find time and energy to write a book. This book would not have been completed without the help of my dear wife, Madhavi, who took care of all my problems and helped me tremendously during the final phases of this endeavor. For this, I will be eternally grateful to her.

I am grateful to all my friends and colleagues who have encouraged me in this endeavor, particularly Navin Goel, Mohan Palat, Vijay Gurbani, Tom Siko, and Gopi Bommakanti. I would like to thank Jim Bennett for his inspiration and perseverance, which seems to have given me some motivation.

I am grateful to my parents, my brother Ravi, and sister Mukta, for all the moral support they have provided me in all my years spent away from home.

I am grateful to all those who made this possible.

Object-Oriented
Paradigm

Introduction

This chapter provides an overview of object-oriented technology (OOT), with special emphasis on the object-oriented programming (OOP) paradigm. It offers an introduction to OOP concepts and OOP terminology. It also offers a brief introduction to popular OOP languages, along with guidelines for selecting an object-oriented language.

1.1 Object-Oriented Programming—The Paradigm Shift

There has been a great change in the fundamental approach to software development over the last two decades, with the emphasis on top-down design and process-oriented structured programming methodology being supplanted by a more flexible and reusable object-oriented approach. This has been termed by some a *paradigm shift*. This shift in the fundamental approach to software development has been a gradual process propelled by the need to create systems that are not only easy to develop and maintain, but also easy to extend. The object-oriented programming paradigm makes it possible to model systems in terms that match human thinking and language. The central themes in the object-oriented approach are the concepts of objects and actions on objects.

1.2 Objects

Objects are representations of real-world entities in the application software domain. Real-world entities can be described in terms of their attributes and behavior. To capture the features and interactions of real-world entities, objects are defined in terms of their attributes and operations. Objects can interact with one another by sending messages to one another. The message-sending paradigm is the means of communication in object-oriented (OO) systems. When an object receives a message from another object, it executes an appropriate method.

Objects that are similar to one another in behavior and other characteristics can be grouped together into a class. This provides a level of abstraction that helps create a generic description and specification for the group of objects. The next level of abstraction is to identify those things that are common in classes that seem similar, and create superclasses, or parent classes, and subclasses. This gives rise to a hierarchy of classes.

Stemple et al.[1] have provided an excellent description of the concept of an object:

> An object is an encapsulated abstract data type, and as such its properties need not be single values, but can be other entities of arbitrary complexity. This allows us to create a one-to-one mapping between objects and entities we are trying to model. A single, real-world entity is represented as a single entity: there is no need to break it up and spread it across relations as would be required in a relational database system, for example. Objects are treated as first-class structures, and can thus be embedded in data structures, passed as parameters, and returned as values.

1.3   Object-Oriented Concepts

Object orientation is the combination of several software engineering concepts, such as encapsulation, information hiding, data abstraction, and modular programming (see Fig. 1.1). These concepts are incorporated into the concepts of objects, classes, and class hierarchies. These software engineering concepts are described below.

Data abstraction: This is an extension of the concept of data types. It allows for the definition of abstract operations on abstract data. The behavior of an abstract data object is completely defined by a set of abstract operations defined on the object.

Information hiding: This is a software design technique that makes it possible to hide the complexity and the implementation details of a module from the clients of the module. This concept is related to encapsulation. In general, information hiding is defined as any programming method which limits the computation allowed by the type system upon data by restricting either the access or the type

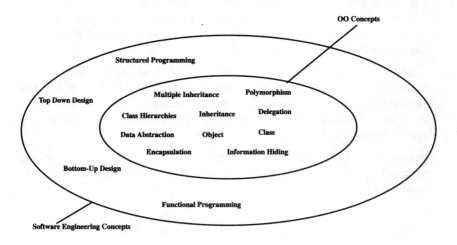

Figure 1.1 Software engineering concepts incorporated into object-oriented paradigm.

interface to it. Information hiding may be relied on as a protection mechanism only within the context of a strong type system.

Encapsulation: This is a software design technique which makes it possible to define a scope for a module of code and its data, in order to limit and control access by the clients of the encapsulated module. A module is encapsulated if clients of the module are restricted by the definition of the programming language to accessing the module only via its defined external interface. The process of combining data and the code relevant to the data, all in one module, so as to restrict access to the object is termed encapsulation. Encapsulation minimizes interdependencies among separately coded modules by defining strict external interfaces. Wills[2] has provided an excellent description of encapsulation in object-oriented programming languages (OOPLs):

> Encapsulation is the idea that the clients of a unit of software design should depend only on its published interface, not its innards: the knock-on effects of a change of implementation stop at the unit's boundaries, provided the interface description remains true. In OOP terms, this means that it is none of a client's business to use a class's internal functions or to see internal data structures.

Object: An object is the encapsulation of data representing some physical entity in the real world, along with operations to manipulate the data. Objects interact with other objects to provide or acquire services. An object is an instance of one class.

Class: Objects that share the same functionality and characteristics can be grouped into a class. A class is a template for objects. It comprises a definition of object behavior and attributes. Objects are considered to be instances of a class.

Class hierarchy: When classes are derived from other classes, they form a tree-structured aggregation of class definitions in which the relationship between two adjacent classes on a branch is expressed by a subclass-superclass relationship. The subclass is considered a specialization of the superclass.

Inheritance: Inheritance is the mechanism of sharing behavior and attributes between classes where one class "is-a" specialization of another class.

In addition, object orientation typically implies the availability of the message-passing paradigm for object communications.

1.4   Object-Oriented Programming (OOP)

Snyder[3] has described object-oriented programming (OOP) as a programming methodology that is based on the following key characteristics:

1. Designers define new classes (or types) of objects.

2. Objects have operations defined on them.

3. Invocations operate on multiple types of objects (i.e., operations are generic).

4. Class definitions share common components using inheritance.

1.5   What Are Object-Oriented Systems?

Systems that are designed using object-oriented concepts of objects, classes, inheritance, polymorphism, and delegation are generally considered to be object-oriented systems. As such, they tend to be composed of reusable components, and are expected to be easily maintainable and extensible.

The following are the characteristics of typical object-oriented systems (see Fig. 1.2):

1. Object identity

2. Data abstraction and encapsulation

3. Classes of data

4. Inheritance

5. Composite and complex objects

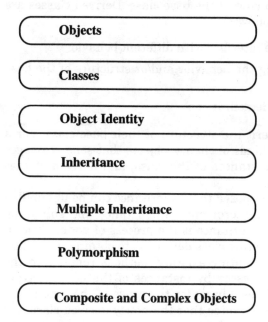

Figure 1.2   Characteristics of OO systems.

6. Polymorphism

1.6   Levels of Object Orientation

Peter Wegner[4] has defined three levels of object orientation for applications:

1. *Object-based:* Object-based languages, tools, and methodologies that support the concept of the object and the message-passing paradigm of object communications.

2. *Class-based:* Systems where the concept of classes is the basis for object orientation. Classes are used as templates for objects.

3. *Object-oriented:* Systems of software which support the pivotal concepts of encapsulation, message passing, dynamic binding, and inheritance.

1.7   Inheritance

Inheritance is the code-sharing mechanism by which a new class of objects can be defined in terms of an existing class, called the *base class.* The classes derived from a base class augment or redefine the existing structure and behavior of the base class. Derived classes are usually employed for the following:[5]

1. Implementing the same interface with different behavior
2. Incrementally extending the behavior and/or structure of the base class
3. Providing different implementations

The derived classes inherit the structure of their base class. For a given class, there are two kinds of clients: objects that send messages to invoke methods upon instances of the class, and derived classes that inherit from the class.

Some researchers have proposed that inheritance can be unbundled into two separate concepts, incremental inheritance and subtyping inheritance.[6] Incremental inheritance is the process of adding "methods and variables" to an existing class definition to obtain a new class definition. The code for evaluating existing methods remains in the old (parent) class and is accessed by instances of the new (derived) class. This technique provides a basis for the reuse of the code of the parent class without any guarantee that the newly derived class will be a specialization of the parent class.

Subtyping inheritance, on the other hand, is a technique for arranging class definitions in a hierarchy, satisfying the condition that members of the subclass are also members of the superclass. It is possible to reliably substitute the subtype for the superclass in a system. Subtyping is thus a limited refinement of the superclass, subject to the substitutability condition being met (see Fig. 1.3).

Inheritance makes other OO features possible. Blair et al. has analyzed the contribution of inheritance to object-oriented systems:[7]

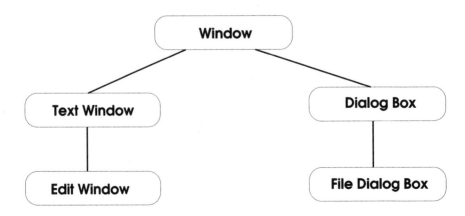

Figure 1.3 Inheritance.

```
OO   Operating systems and networks
OO   Interface and 4GL tools
OO   Languages
OO   Class libraries
OO   Analysis and design tools
OO   Methodologies for OOA and OOD
OODBMSs
```

1. *Inheritance:* The ability to create new classes as specializations of existing classes

2. *Various forms of specialization:* New classes created out of old classes by the addition, redefinition, or deletion of behavior

3. *Class hierarchies:* Classes formed into hierarchies as a result of class specialization

4. *Method binding:* Mapping carried out from method names onto implementations by searching the class hierarchy

5. *Polymorphism:* Methods defined over more than one class either through inheritance or by name overloading

Polymorphism is described in detail in the next section.

1.8 Polymorphism

Polymorphism is used to describe the ability to send a general-purpose message to several objects that will handle them in their own special way (see Fig. 1.4). The details of an object's response to a

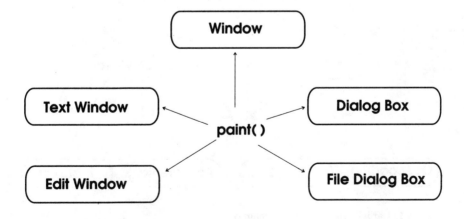

Figure 1.4 Polymorphism.

generic message are subjective to the object. The client sending the message does not have to specify the type of the object to which the message is addressed. Dynamic binding is used to determine the object type at run time to invoke the appropriate implementation of the method for the message.

It is possible to introduce polymorphism into an OO environment in two ways:

1. By means of subclassing, where a method defined on one particular class is automatically defined on all its subclasses

2. By means of overloading, where the same name is used for methods in independent parts of a class hierarchy and hence causes the overloading of the meaning of the term

Polymorphism makes method binding more complex than a straightforward one-to-one mapping. In the presence of polymorphism, method mapping becomes a one-to-many mapping of a method name onto implementations.

Cardelli and Wegner have provided the following taxonomy of polymorphic techniques (see Fig. 1.5):[8]

> Polymorphism can be broadly divided into *universal* polymorphism and *ad hoc* polymorphism. Universal polymorphism, in turn, can be broken down into *parametric* polymorphism and *inclusion* polymorphism. Ad hoc polymorphism can be broken down into *overloading* and *coercion*.

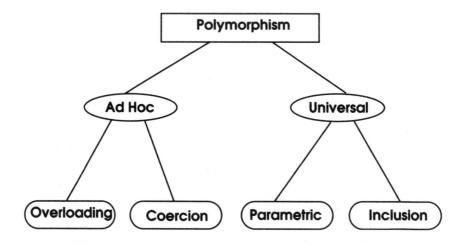

Figure 1.5 Cardelli and Wegner's taxonomy.

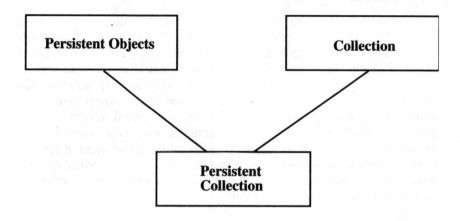

Figure 1.6 Multiple inheritance.

1.9 Multiple Inheritance

Multiple inheritance is the ability to inherit behavior and attributes from more than one superclass (see Fig. 1.6). This implies that such classes can be classified in several ways simultaneously. An example of multiple inheritance is a class of listboxes that need to inherit the functionality of windows from a class of display windows, as well as the functionality of an ordered collection from a class of ordered collections.

1.10 Class-Based vs. Classless Object Orientation

Object-oriented systems can be broadly categorized into class-based OO systems and classless OO systems. In class-based OO systems, a class is considered to be a template for objects, and objects are considered to be instances of their classes. Inheritance is the mechanism for code sharing. A subclass inherits behavior and attributes from a superclass.

Classless OO systems are also called delegation-based systems. Delegation is another mechanism for sharing functionality and code in OO systems. It is an alternative to inheritance. An object can have some of its functionality delegated to it from other objects. Code sharing is thus not limited to classes involved in superclass-subclass relationships.

1.11   Delegation

Delegation is an alternative to inheritance as an information-sharing mechanism. Using delegation, references to an attribute of an object (the "child" object in such a sharing relationship) can be rerouted to another object (the "parent"). The child object thus inherits certain behavior from its parent object, and the relationship between the objects is not one of subclass-superclass type. Some experimental systems have employed delegation for its conceptual simplicity and greater flexibility. For example, the Dynamo system developed at the University of Southern California has been designed using a form of inheritance characterized as *incremental multiple inheritance by delegation*. Data attributes may be delegated as well as code, allowing objects to share data and behavior.

1.12   Availability of OO Technology and Applications

Some of the OO technologies (packaged in some form) that are being used to develop software application products are

- Case tools based on OOT
- Analysis and design tools, some with OO capabilities
- Knowledge-based systems
- Hypermedia, Hypertext
- GUI front ends
- Object DBMS
- Rapid application development environments

In the commercial CASE environments, vendors are employing OOT for all their products. GUI tools are mostly designed using OO concepts, and classes of GUI tools are widely available.

1.13   Object-Oriented Programming Languages (OOPLs)

The following is a list of some popular OOPLs:

- C++ Language System
- C_Talk
- Smalltalk/V
- Smalltalk-80

- Actor
- Enfin
- ProKappa
- Eiffel
- KnowledgePro
- Classic-Ada with Persistence
- Objective-C
- Trellis/Owl
- Flavors
- CLOS
- CommonLoops

Most OOPLs can trace their origins to Simula. The concepts of objects and classes are employed by most of these languages. A brief description of some of these languages is provided in this chapter.

1.14 Simula

Simula is a programming language that was developed in the late 1960s for use in computer simulations and modeling. Simula was an improvement on Algol-60, and included the ideas of classes and inheritance. In Simula, all objects belong to classes. Objects are given identifiers indicating their classes, and they can have a set of attributes. Objects can have an action sequence that will be executed when the object is created.

1.15 Smalltalk

Smalltalk is perhaps the oldest OOPL. It features a pure form of object-oriented programming. Smalltalk provides a modeless software development environment, using windows, pop-up menus, and a mouse-based user interface. Smalltalk also provides its own set of reusable software components, which can be used as building blocks for creating new user applications. In Smalltalk, the algorithms that determine an object's behavior and performance are called *methods*. When a message is sent to an object, a method is evaluated, and an object is returned as a result.

Classes are also considered to be objects in Smalltalk. Class objects belong to a class called the *metaclass*. The metaclass determines the messages to which the class can respond. There are three important classes relating to metaclasses:

1. Metaclass: the class of all metaclasses.
2. Class: the superclass of all instances of Metaclass.
3. Every metaclass has exactly one instance: the class of which it is the metaclass.

Smalltalk is a language that was intended to be used in the context of a comprehensive programming environment that provided a wide range of tools for manipulating and understanding programs.

1.16 Common LISP Object System (CLOS)

CLOS is an OO extension to Common LISP. In CLOS, objects contain slots instead of instance variables. Methods that act on objects are defined separately from the objects, and are accessed by a functional syntax: (method object) denotes applying the method method to the object object. CLOS incorporates the concept of *generic functions* to permit different methods to be associated with different objects. Methods, in CLOS, exist independently of objects. Each CLOS method is regarded as belonging to a generic function.

In CLOS, specific instances of a class can have some behavior independent of their class. Classes in CLOS are first-class objects, and can be manipulated like any other objects. Thus classes can be dynamically created. CLOS provides support for multiple inheritance.

1.17 Objective-C

Objective-C is considered by some researchers to be a cross between C and Smalltalk. It is possible to precompile Objective-C code to produce standard C as output. Objective-C incorporates the concept of an object identifier, *id,* which is a handle for referring to an object in a *message expression.* Object-C is a compiled language, unlike Smalltalk and CLOS.

1.18 C++

C++ is the most popular OOPL. It is an object-oriented extension to C, developed at AT&T Bell Laboratories. C++ supports the OOP concepts of objects, classes, inheritance, multiple inheritance, polymorphism, and parameterized types. The C++ class concept can be considered as the generalization of the C feature of a *struct.*

C++ has been evolving since it was first released by AT&T as a version of C with classes in 1984. The latest release is version 3.1, and provides multiple inheritance, type-safe linkages, abstract classes, and a form of exception handling.

C++ provides an access control mechanism for the operations on objects. The operations are called *member functions*. Member functions can have one of the following three modes of access:

- Public
- Private
- Protected

Public member functions are accessible by all clients of the object. Private member functions are accessible only by other member functions of the class. Protected member functions are accessible only by other member functions and the member functions of classes derived from that class.

Snyder[9] has summarized the model of C++ objects in the following points:

- Class instances are objects.
- Pointers to class instances are object names.
- Pointers reveal object identity to clients.
- Base components of derived class instances are not objects.
- Public data members correspond to special operations that return pointers.
- All function invocations are request forms, except for invocations that suppress virtual function lookup, which are direct method invocations.
- Except for virtual functions, each function is a distinct operation.
- An overriding virtual function is a new method for one or more existing operations.
- Virtual functions are generic operations; overloaded functions are not.
- C++ values of nonclass types are values (request parameters).
- C++ nonclass types are types.
- Subtyping is defined between pointer types based on class derivation.
- A class whose members are pure virtual functions is an interface.
- A pointer type to an interface class is an interface type.
- Operations are values.
- A C++ function type is an operation signature.

1.19 Actor

Actor is an OOPL that is derived from the OO research done in Smalltalk and other OOPLs. The Actor programming environment provides about 150 classes in the class library and comes with a resource toolkit which provides visual editing capabilities. Programmers usually create new classes in the Actor environment by deriving them from classes that already exist in Actor. This is in line with one of the main goals of OOP, that of minimizing the amount of new code that must be written for a particular task.

While polymorphism allows the class of the receiver of a message to take on different values at run time, the `perform` message in Actor allows the message selector itself to be computed at run time. This can eliminate yet another layer of control structure, creating a clean, data-driven approach to programming.

Actor's development tools are essentially pop-up windows for compiling code, inspecting objects, and debugging code.

1.20 Comparing OOPLs

Different OOPLs are appropriate for different environments. Kahn is convinced that Smalltalk is better than C++ for corporate environments:[10] "We think Smalltalk is a great development language for the corporate developer. We think it's better than C++ because it's a higher level language. We think Smalltalk will be the Cobol of the OO world in the future."

In Smalltalk, objects are used to represent every value in the system, including primitive values like numbers and boolean. In CLOS, most values can be treated as objects. Objective-C and C++ provide all values provided in C, and in addition provide a separate domain of objects.

In C++, classes are used as templates for objects. They are compile entities and have no representation as objects at run time. In Smalltalk and CLOS, classes are first-class objects, and can be treated just like any other object. They can be dynamically created. In Objective-C, classes do have a representation at run time, but their representation is created statically by the compiler and cannot be dynamically created.

Smalltalk, Flavors, and Objective-C allow free access to inherited instance variables by descendant classes. Other OOPLs, like C++, restrict access to inherited instance variables. Where access to inherited instance variables is needed, it should be provided in the form of operations. Only CLOS permits specific instances of classes to have behavior independent of their classes.

1.21   Choosing an OOPL

Choosing an OOPL for software development is not an easy task. Many detailed aspects of each language must be evaluated based on a number of criteria. An exhaustive and complete comparison of languages based on OO concepts would be a huge undertaking. Languages must be evaluated on the basis of *syntax, semantics,* and *pragmatics.*

The syntax for invoking an operation on an object is an important part of evaluation. Languages like C++ have syntax similar to other structured languages, and adopt a conventional-looking procedure call or function syntax.

Cook[11] has compared the semantic aspects of OOPLs on the following 11 dimensions:

1. *Objects and values:* Do some expressions in the language denote objects and other expressions denote other kinds of values, or do all expressions uniformly denote objects?

2. *Class and instances:* Do all objects belong to a class?

3. *Inheritance:* What kind of inheritance is provided?

4. *Self-reference:* How does the language provide for making reference to the current object?

5. *Type system:* Does the language have a type system? Does type checking take place prior to execution?

6. *Object initialization:* What facilities are provided for initializing the state of objects when they are created?

7. *Encapsulation, scoping, and hiding:* Which textual contexts can variables and methods be accessed from? Does the language provide mechanisms for explicitly controlling scope?

8. *Methods, binding, and polymorphism:* Are methods regarded as part of objects or as separate entities? Can methods be overridden when inherited, and what are the rules for doing this?

9. *Control structure:* Are control structures, sequential or otherwise, built into the language or constructed from lower-level primitives?

10. *Concurrency:* Are objects concurrent?

11. *Metalevel programming:* To what extent are the language's features programmed in the language itself? Does it have metaclasses or other kinds of metaobjects?

The pragmatic issues of OOPLs are hard to define precisely. It is important to focus on issues of programming environments, support for software development, the nature of the language (interpretive or compiled), and the use of garbage collection facilities. Other pragmatic issues are the unit of modularity, support for error handling, and the incorporation of any specific software development methodology in the language.

Madsen[12] has suggested that languages employed to implement OOD must support object orientation directly, and should support

1. Modeling of concepts and phenomena—i.e., the language must include constructs like class, type, and procedure.

2. Modeling classification hierarchies—i.e., subclassing (inheritance) and virtuals.

3. Modeling active objects—i.e., concurrency and coroutine sequencing, combined with persistency.

1.22   Class Categories in C++

C++ is the most popular OOPL to date. It is therefore important to explore the C++ object model in some detail. In this section, the support for object classification in C++ is reviewed.

When classes are designed, they can be designed to be one of several possible kinds of classes. Each kind of class is better suited for expressing certain design ideas. Booch and Vilot[13] have identified five kinds of classes in C++:

1. Concrete data types

2. Abstract data types

3. Node classes

4. Interface classes

5. Handle classes

Abstract data types are used to identify the set of values and a relevant set of operations on those values without regard to how these values are represented. Pure virtual functions in C++ help make the class an abstract class. Concrete data types, in contrast to abstract data types, are considered to be a complete implementation of a class, incorporating both the interface and the representation of the class, and often do not use other classes.

A node class is typically used to provide a framework for other classes. These are usually classes derived from other classes, and in turn serve as base classes to other classes. Node classes are usually members of a class hierarchy that can be used not only to create objects but also to create other classes by inheritance. Interface classes are used to provide compile-time type adjustments, as in a class that encapsulates type casting needed in container classes based on generic pointers. Handle classes can be used to provide an interface with only a minimal representation. The actual representation of the object can be handled by another class. Handle classes are a special form of interface classes.

1.23 Class Libraries

Software development in OOP environments is faster than in traditional environments because of the availability of class libraries that provide a core set of classes from which the application is assembled. The classes that developers create should also be arranged in reusable class libraries. Leinfuss[10] has provided the following tips for writing class libraries, originally credited to John Williams:

1. Keep methods coherent. Let them perform a single function.
2. Keep them small. They should not be larger than two pages. Don't try to do too much in a method.
3. Establish standards to keep methods consistent. Function overloading helps provide some consistency in naming.
4. Separate policy from implementation methods.
5. Provide uniform coverage for a method. Write methods for all combinations of input.
6. Broaden the method as much as possible, generalizing the argument types.
7. Avoid global information. Minimize external references.
8. Avoid modes. Behaviors based on modes that represent contexts limit reusability.
9. Be careful when naming conventions. For example, do not name a class with a string, as that name is used with the X Windows system. Give class names that are unique.

It is better to build very shallow trees of classes in libraries, as maintenance can be a problem with deep hierarchies.

1.24 The Necessity for Formal Methods in OOP

OOP makes it possible to build systems rapidly using widely distributed and adapted components. Designers who use prepackaged software components need to be able to fully comprehend the features and limitations of those components. Thus, it is desirable to provide the required behavioral characteristics of a software component in unambiguous language. It is also desirable to be able to check each reusable component against its requirements.

Wills[2] has focused on this problem in his research, and has suggested three good reasons why behavioral specifications are more necessary in the OOP software engineering paradigm than in a more traditional one:

1. With parts acquired from everywhere, the designer must be especially careful to have an unambiguous understanding of what each part is supposed to do, and some guarantee that it will indeed do it. If you have to test each part just as carefully as if you'd built it yourself, much of the advantage of reusability is lost.

2. Furthermore, if updated versions of a component are to be distributed and incorporated into systems which use it, the systems' designer must be able to distinguish those features of the component's behavior which are incidental from those which will be retained in future versions.

3. Lastly, polymorphic code generally requires the types with which it deals (or is instantiated) to conform to some restrictions. It is insufficient to check that objects passed to a sorting routine all accept the binary operator "<"; additionally, "<" must work like a proper ordering on them. In a closed system which is all written by one designer, it may be acceptable to document these restrictions informally or not at all, but where polymorphic code is to be distributed widely for use in conjunction with classes its designers have never conceived of, it is important both that the precise constraints on client classes are documented and that the code is guaranteed to work with any client class which conforms to those constraints. Otherwise, again, the client designers might as well build and test the distributed code for themselves.

1.25 Benefits of OOP

There are several benefits of adopting OOP. The following three benefits, although subjective, are considered by many to be major reasons for adopting OOP:[12]

1. Programs reflect reality.

2. The model is more stable than functionality.

3. Subclassing and virtuals improve the reusability of code.

1.26   Transition to OOT

OOT has the reputation of requiring a steep learning curve. This is due not only to the necessity of learning a new language, but also to the necessity of unlearning process-oriented programming techniques. Because of the differences between top-down structured programming and the OO techniques, the transition from a traditional structured programming environment to an object-oriented environment requires a high investment of time and energy.

There are several reasons for the lack of enthusiasm for adopting OOP in most MIS departments. Capers Jones[10] notes, "OOP languages are not widely used for MIS because of the culture and the need to deal with legacy software written in Cobol."

References

1. David Stemple, Adolfo Socoro, and Tim Sheard, "Formalizing Objects for Database using ADABTPL," in *Lecture Notes in Computer Science, Advances in Object-Oriented Database Systems, 2nd International Workshop on Object-Oriented Database Systems,* Springer-Verlag, 1988.
2. Alan Wills, "Capsules and Types in Fresco: Program verification in Smalltalk," in Pierre America (ed.), *Lecture Notes in Computer Science, ECOOP '91, European Conference on Object-Oriented Programming,* Springer-Verlag, 1991.
3. Alan Snyder, "Encapsulation and Inheritance in Object-Oriented Programming Languages," *OOPSLA '86 Proceedings,* September 1986, pp. 38–45.
4. Peter Wegner, "Concepts and Paradigms of Object-Oriented Programming," *OOPS Messenger,* Vol. 1, No. 1, August 1990, pp. 25–27.
5. Grady Booch and Michael Vilot, "Object-Oriented Design: Inheritance Relationships," *C++ Report,* vol. 2, no. 9, 1990, pp. 8–11.
6. Elspeth Cusack, "Inheritance in Object-Oriented Z," in Pierre America (ed.), *Lecture Notes in Computer Science, ECOOP '91, European Conference on Object-Oriented Programming,* Springer-Verlag, 1991.
7. Gordon S. Blair, Howard Bowman, and Rodger Lea, "Basic Concepts I (Objects, Classes and Inheritance)," in Gordon Blair, John Gallagher, David Hutchinson, and Doug Sheperd (eds.), *Object-Oriented Languages, Systems and Applications,* Halsted Press, Ottawa, 1990.
8. L. Cardelli and P. Wegner, "On Understanding Types, Data Abstraction, and Polymorphism," *Computing Surveys,* vol. 17, no. 4, 1985, pp. 471–522.
9. Alan Snyder, "Modeling the C++ Object Model: An Application of an Abstract Object Model," in Pierre America (ed.), *Lecture Notes in Computer Science, ECOOP '91, European Conference on Object-Oriented Programming,* Springer-Verlag, 1991.
10. Emily Leinfuss, "Managing Class Libraries Takes Discipline," *Software Magazine,* Client/Server Computing Special Edition, January 1993.
11. Stephen J. Cook, "Programming Languages Based on Objects," in Gordon Blair, John Gallagher, David Hutchinson, and Doug Sheperd (eds.), *Object-Oriented Languages, Systems and Applications,* Halsted Press, 1990.
12. Ole Lehrmann Madsen, "Basic Principles of the BETA Programming Language," in Gordon Blair, John Gallagher, David Hutchinson, and Doug Sheperd (eds.), *Object-Oriented Languages, Systems and Applications,* Halsted Press, 1990.
13. Grady Booch and Michael Vilot, "Object-Oriented Design: C++ Class Categories," *C++ Report,* vol. 3, no. 7, 1991, pp. 6–10.

Object-Oriented Methodologies

Introduction

This chapter provides an overview of object-oriented analysis and design methodologies. It offers an introduction to some of the popular object-oriented analysis (OOA) and design (OOD) methodologies that have become widely used in recent years.

2.1 Traditional Approaches to Software Design and Development

The structured analysis/structured design (SA/SD) approach has been employed for software analysis and design for over two decades, and can be considered to be representative of traditional approaches to software development. The structured analysis phase has traditionally employed some of the following:

1. Data flow diagrams
2. The data dictionary
3. State transition diagrams
4. Entity-relationship (ER) diagrams

The structured design phase involves grouping the processes from the data flow diagrams into tasks and converting the tasks into programming language functions.

2.2   James Rumbaugh's OMT Approach

The OMT methodology employs three kinds of models as part of the information model of the system: the *object model,* describing the objects in the system and their relationships; the *dynamic model,* describing the interactions among objects in the system; and the *functional model,* describing the data transformations of the system.[1] These three models are considered as orthogonal views of the system.

An object model is created as the first step in analyzing the problem. As part of the object model, classes are defined, even for objects that may be unique within a particular context. While identifying objects in the problem context and highlighting classes of such objects, specifying container classes as part of the analysis phase must be avoided. Object diagrams are created to express the associations among objects. A data dictionary accompanies every object diagram. The data dictionary contains descriptions of every class and provides detailed information on all class attributes and operations. It also provides information on associations among classes. Object diagrams are improved with attributes and inheritance.

Defining the object model is an iterative process, and getting it right might take several passes. The OMT notation has the ability to generalize on several orthogonal dimensions simultaneously. This is done by grouping together all the superclass-subclass relationships on a given dimension into a single generalization object. An actual concrete class involves a subclass from each generalization.[2]

The dynamic model is employed to specify temporal considerations. The sequences of events, the states of events, and the operations that are important are all included in the dynamic model. The dynamic model is important for applications where the user interface makes the application "event-driven." User-interaction sequences are created, and their effect on objects is described in the form of state diagrams. Events that initiate interactions between objects are also identified.

State diagrams can be drawn for each class. For command-driven applications, the commands may be thought of as events on the user interface object. During the object-oriented analysis phase, it is not necessary to create a precise list of commands. During the subsequent design phase, the user interface is modeled by an elaborate state diagram.

The functional model is represented by data flow diagrams (DFD), where the processes correspond to activities or actions on classes, and the flows correspond to objects or attribute values in an object diagram. Thus, the DFDs are used to express functional dependencies among attribute values of objects.

The object design phase of software development that follows the object-oriented analysis phase incorporates design approaches to minimize execution time, memory, and other measures of cost. The object design phase is when the operations identified during analysis must be expressed as algorithms, and when the classes, attributes, and associations from analysis must be implemented as appropriate data structures.

2.3   The Shlaer-Mellor Approach to Object-Oriented Modeling

The objects are identified by abstracting like things in the problem context. The attributes of objects are chosen such that the attributes support the ideas of likeness. An object is defined as an abstraction of a set of real-world things such that all of the real-world things in the set (the instances) have the same characteristics.[3]

The Shlaer-Mellor information model describes

- Objects
- Attributes of those objects
- Relationships between objects

The information model provides the following graphical descriptions of the model:

- Information structure diagram, which is somewhat related to ER diagrams
- Overview information structure diagram, which is a simplified version of the information structure diagram where the attribute names are omitted from the diagram for simplicity and ease of presentation

In addition to the graphical deliverables, the Shlaer-Mellor information model incorporates the following textual forms:

- An object specification document that specifies the entire information model in text. A specification is provided for every object in the model.
- A relationship specification document to describe each relationship in the model.
- A summary specification that can be used as a ready-reference sheet.

The Shlaer-Mellor model employs the terminology of relational databases to implement an object-oriented model. It promotes object orientation as an extension to the relational model.

2.4 The Wirfs-Brock Approach to OOD

Rebecca Wirfs-Brock has proposed a unique methodology using the *responsibility-driven* approach that can be used effectively for OOA and OOD. The main tool that facilitates the preliminary phases of OOA is a deck of cards called the *index cards,* one card per class. The index cards are used to record classes, superclasses, and other relevant details as different phases of OOA and OOD help define the models.

Responsibilities of objects include two key items:[4]

1. The knowledge an object maintains
2. The actions an object can perform

Responsibilities of each object can be identified by answers to the following two questions:

1. What does each object have to do in order to accomplish each goal it is involved with?
2. What steps towards accomplishing each goal is it responsible for?

Objects play the role of clients sometimes, wherein they need services of other objects. At other times, they can play the role of servers, wherein they provide services to other objects. A *contract* between two classes represents a list of services an instance of one class can request from an instance of the other class. Each object can take part in many different contracts. The *responsibilities* of an object are all the services it provides for all the contracts it supports. A contract defines a cohesive set of responsibilities that a client can depend on.[4] Each responsibility will be part of one contract at the most. All responsibilities need to be part of a contract. Some responsibilities are *private* and cannot be requested by other objects.

Collaborations represent requests from a client to a server object in fulfillment of a client responsibility. A collaboration is the embodiment of the contract between a client and a server. An object can fulfill a particular responsibility itself, or it may require the assistance of other objects. An object is considered to collaborate with another if, to fulfill a responsibility, it needs to send the other object any messages. Each collaboration works to fulfill one responsibility. A responsibility may take several collaborations to complete. Identifying collaborations helps highlight the roles played by classes, as clients and servers, in providing the necessary set of system features.

Collaborations can be identified by asking the following questions:

1. Is the class capable of fulfilling this responsibility?
2. If not, what does it need?

3. From what other class can it acquire what it needs?

The OOA phase involves

- Identifying abstract and concrete classes
- Building hierarchy graphs that illustrate inheritance relationships between classes
- Drawing Venn diagrams representing the responsibilities shared between classes
- Constructing contracts defined by each class

2.5 Seven-Step Approach to OOD

Schultz has proposed a seven-step approach to OOD:[5]

1. Identify candidate objects. This can be facilitated by the creation of one or more model objects and extracting their interrelationships.

2. Identify operations suffered by and required of each object. This step involves extracting the operations of interest from the models created during OOA. This might involve eliminating all unnecessary object coupling while preserving necessary application-specific coupling. This step also addresses assumptions made about the environment.

3. Select, create, and verify objects. Information about each object is gathered, and decisions are made about reusing existing objects or creating new ones. At this point in the design, reusing source code is not the issue. It is too early to address reusability. This step addresses the non-programming-language-specific specifications for objects. Object and class specifications (OCS) are used. Classes and objects are generalized so as to be reusable.

4. Implementation issues are addressed. Source-code implementations are considered explicitly. In this step, decisions must be made concerning whether an individual object should be implemented as a class, a metaclass, a parameterized class, an abstract class, or a nonclass instance. Public interfaces to the objects are also addressed.

5. OO graphical models are created. One or more graphical representations are produced based on decisions made in the previous step. A software architecture is created.

6. The interfaces to each object are established. Programming-language interfaces to the objects are created for objects that make up the interfaces to the major system components.

7. Each object is implemented and simple objects are coded. For complex objects that form a major system component, it may be necessary to apply the entire design process to that component recursively.

The first three steps are language-independent. The last four may involve a programming language. It is important to approach the last four steps with parallel thinking, to address the issues with as much language-independence as possible.

Object and class specification are very critical to the design effort. They provides an external, high-level, language-independent view of the object. Some of the objects defined by an OCS may just be logical models and may never be implemented in code. Each OCS is divided into five sections:

1. A precise and concise description

2. The graphical representation of the object

3. Both suffered and required operations for the object

4. A description of the state information associated with the object

5. Descriptions of any exported constants and exceptions to the object

Suffered operations are those that are advertised to the world and that change or query the state of the object in which they are encapsulated. Required operations are those operations suffered by objects other than the encapsulating object, and are required by the encapsulating object to ensure the desired and correct characteristics of the encapsulating object.

2.6 Using Relationship between Objects

Objects interacting in a system make use of the services offered by other objects. The *using* relationship can be used to express a subset of such interactions. Booch and Vilot[6] have identified three roles that each object may play in using relationships:

Actor objects can operate upon other objects, but are never operated upon by other objects. Such objects make use of services offered by other objects but do not themselves provide any service to the objects they make use of.

Server objects never operate upon other objects, but are only operated upon by other objects.

Agent objects can both operate upon other objects and be operated upon by other objects.

2.7   Containing Relationships between Objects

Quite often, objects that contain other objects need to be represented in such a way that they are logically regarded as a single object. It is important to provide for *containing* relationships by which the composite logical object can refer to the contained objects. Typically, the contained objects are treated as private objects of the enclosing object. This encapsulation might not be appropriate if such a tight coupling is not desired.

2.8   Relationships among Classes

Rumbaugh[7] has identified three types of class relationships:

- Generalization, or "kind-of"
- Aggregation, or "part-of"
- Association, implying some semantic connection

Booch and Vilot[6] have identified two more types of relationships between classes:

- Instantiation relationships
- Metaclass relationships

Booch and Vilot suggest the following rule of thumb for identifying relationships: "If an abstraction is more than the sum of its component parts, then using relationships are more appropriate. If an abstraction is a kind of some other abstraction or if that abstraction is exactly equal to the sum of its components, then inheritance is a better approach."

2.9   OO Design vs. Bottom-Up vs. Top-Down Methods

OO design is typically based on the concepts of objects and classes. Unlike structured design methodology, OO design methodologies typically begin by identifying the objects that are available in the environment and then proceeding to classify them. Rather than decomposition based on the various functions and features of the application, objects from which a system is built model both the data and related operations corresponding to parts of the overall system.

Unlike many other approaches to design, it is not possible to categorize OOD as fundamentally top-down or bottom-up.[8] It includes both approaches. When a designer is reusing an existing object or class, it can be considered to be a bottom-up approach. However, when decomposing a large design into the smaller elements which will be subsequently mapped onto objects and classes, the approach can be considered to be top-down.

Booch and Vilot[9] consider the shortcomings of traditional development methods to be the following:

- They don't address data abstraction and information hiding.
- They are inadequate for problems with concurrency.
- They are often not responsive to changes in the problem.

In the presence of inheritance, a major issue that is usually encountered is that of the relationships between classifications. In some approaches, the relationships are *implicit,* and relationships exist between classifications because they share common behavior. In other approaches, the relationships between classifications are *explicit,* and are specified by the programmer. The implicit relationship approach is considered by some researchers to be similar to the top-down design of computer systems, whereas the explicit approach is considered to mirror a bottom-up approach. Blair[10] has made the following observations:

> In top-down design methodologies, it is common that designers describe in full the behavior of objects without consideration of the implementation. Abstract data types are often used for this process. In bottom-up methodologies, however, classifications are created out of existing classifications until a target environment is established. Classes and inheritance are often proposed as an ideal vehicle for bottom-up design. Therefore, by implementing both abstract data types and classes in an object-oriented language, it is possible to marry the advantages of top-down and bottom-up design. An implicit style of polymorphism can be used with abstract data types to preserve the full specification of objects and an explicit approach can be used with classes to introduce an element of reuse.

2.10 Modeling Relationships in C++

Interactions between objects can be captured during OOD by appropriate relationships. At the implementation level, C++ provides the following mechanisms for implementing object relationships:[9]

1. Global objects
2. Function arguments
3. Constructors
4. Base classes
5. Templates

2.11   Comparing OO Models

The OMT model is similar to SA/SD to the extent that both methodologies support three orthogonal views of a system—the object, dynamic, and function models. However, in the SA/SD approach, the functional model is emphasized, and the object model is not considered as important as the other two. In Rumbaugh's OMT model, the object model is considered to be the most important, and the functional model the least important. The OMT approach, like other OO approaches, emphasizes the decomposition of the application domain based on objects of the real world, while the SA/SD approach takes an arbitrary approach to decomposition, as there is no single standard technique for decomposition of processes into subprocesses.

Comparing his OMT approach to other OO approaches, Rumbaugh has made the following claims:[1]

> A major distinction between Booch's approach and the OMT approach is the emphasis we place on associations. Booch mentions associations in referring to our past work but has not truly incorporated them into his methodology. The similarities between the approaches are more striking than the differences, and both approaches complement each other. Shlaer and Mellor's methodology, like our OMT methodology, breaks analysis down into three phases: static modeling of objects, dynamic modeling of states and events, and functional modeling. All in all, we think that their methodology is quite good. A flaw with Shlaer and Mellor's treatment is their excessive preoccupation with relational database tables and database keys.

Researchers at Hewlett-Packard have conducted a study of the differences between OO methods. The popular OO methods were evaluated by scoring them against a set of criteria expressed as a set of questions,[11] some of which are listed below:

1. Is the method class-based or package-based? Does it support generic modules and/or metaclasses?

2. What type of inheritance does the method support?

3. What visibility relationships does the method support?

4. Does the method support object creation and destruction?

5. Does the method support object persistence?

6. What models of concurrency does the method support?

7. What models of communication does the method support?

8. What models does the method prescribe, and what notation is used for each? Are there any aspects of a system that are omitted or any that are covered by more than one model?

9. Is the method's notation appropriately expressive?

10. Is there a syntax definition, or does the syntax have to be deduced from examples?

11. Does the semantics have a formal definition?

12. Does the notation provide a partitioning mechanism?

13. Are there rules for composing the meaning of a system from the meaning of its modules?

14. Does the process provide support for adding functionality to existing systems and reengineering?

15. Does the process address the issue of design with reuse?

16. Does the process address the issue of design for reuse?

17. Which of the following activities does the process support: analysis, design, and implementation?

18. Are the process steps well defined? Is the process flexible?

19. What resources are available to support the method? Are there CASE tools available to support the method?

20. Is the method targeted at a specific language?

The OO methodologies studied as part of the evaluations were the following:

- Booch
- Buhr
- HOOD
- Rumbaugh
- Wirfs-Brock

The HP study concluded that the Booch, Rumbaugh, and Wirfs-Brock methodologies fully support OO concepts. Both the HOOD and the Buhr methodologies are package-based and omit inheritance. The Rumbaugh notations are concise, some of them borrowed from SA/SD. The Wirfs-Brock methodology helps exploratory analysis and informal design, and might prove useful for analysis or high-end design.

References

1. James Rumbaugh, Michael Blaha, William Premerlani, Frederick Eddy, and William Lorensen, *Object-Oriented Modeling and Design,* Prentice-Hall, Englewood Cliffs, N.J., 1991.
2. James Rumbaugh, "An Object or Not an Object?" *Journal of Object-Oriented Programming,* vol. 5, no. 3, 1992, pp. 20–25.
3. Sally Shlaer and Stephen J. Mellor, *Object-Oriented Systems Analysis,* Yourden Press Computing Series, Englewood Cliffs, N.J., 1988.

4. Rebecca Wirfs-Brock, Brian Wilkerson, and Lauren Weiner, *Designing Object-Oriented Software,* Prentice-Hall, Englewood Cliffs, N.J., 1990, pp. 62–63.

5. Ron Schultz, "A Game Plan for OOD Developers," *Open Systems Today,* Sept. 21, 1992.

6. Grady Booch and Michael Vilot, "Object-Oriented Design: Object and Class Relationships," *C++ Report,* vol. 2, no. 5, 1990, pp. 10–12.

7. James Rumbaugh, "Relational Database Design Using an Object-Oriented Methodology," *Communications of the ACM,* vol. 31, no. 4, 1988, p. 417.

8. Andrew Ormsby, "Object-Oriented Design Methods," in Gordon Blair, John Gallagher, David Hutchinson, and Doug Shepherd, (eds.) *Object-Oriented Languages, Systems and Applications,* Halsted Press, 1990.

9. Grady Booch and Michael Vilot, "Connecting Objects," *C++ Report,* vol. 3, no. 1, 1991, pp. 10–13.

10. Gordon Blair, "What Are Object-Oriented Systems?" in Gordon Blair, John Gallagher, David Hutchinson, and Doug Shepherd (eds.), *Object-Oriented Languages, Systems and Applications,* Halsted Press, 1990.

11. Patrick Arnold, Stephanie Bodoff, Derek Coleman, Helena Gilchrist, and Fiona Hayes, "An Evaluation of Five Object-Oriented Development Methods," Technical Report HPL-91-52, Hewlett-Packard, June 1991.

3

Relational Databases and OODBMS

Introduction

This chapter focuses on the differences between traditional, namely relational, approaches to database applications and the object-oriented approach to database applications. The impedance mismatch problem and other issues highlighting the inadequacies of relational technology for storing and retrieving n-dimensional data are explained in detail.

3.1 Database Applications

There are two categories of database applications: those that involve storing large amounts of mostly static data, such as parts information in an inventory system, and those that are process-intensive and involve complex dynamic data, such as engineering data, where the structure of the data is intertwined closely with the structure of the program. Traditional (relational and hierarchical) databases are well equipped to manage static data for relatively simple applications where the structure of the data remains mostly static after the data analysis. In such applications, once the database has been set up, the schema does not evolve much over time. Conventional databases provide data persistence, mechanisms for data sharing, and data security (see Fig. 3.1).

The central concepts of relational systems are

1. The disaggregation of data stored in the database. This is what normalizations are all about.

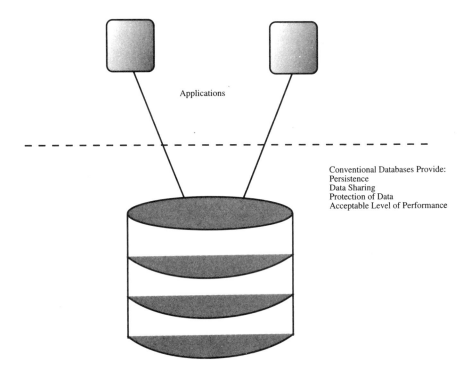

Figure 3.1 Conventional databases.

2. Separate reaggregations of data as needed by each application that uses the database. This takes place in the form of joins of data across tables.

3. Set-at-a-time treatment of records.

Relational databases are designed so that there is a strict separation between data and programs that use the data.

3.2   Functions Expected of Conventional Databases

Conventional database models provide adequate support for applications where the structure of the database tends to be fairly static once the large files of records are set up. Such databases typically need to provide the following:

- Persistence of data
- Data sharing
- Protection of data

- Acceptable levels of performance

OODBs have to provide all the features listed above, and a lot more features demanded by complex applications that are not currently met by conventional database systems. The strengths of conventional databases, especially relational DBMSs, can be summarized as follows:[1]

1. Suitability for online transaction processing
2. Performance with large amounts of structurally regular data
3. A more or less mathematically tractable data model
4. Industry standard data definition and data manipulation languages that are more or less adhered to
5. A large body of experience and knowledge in the data management community

3.3 Where Conventional Databases Fail to Deliver

For applications where the scheme of the data is likely to change, and where the data are complex or n-dimensional, conventional databases are usually not flexible enough or efficient enough (see Fig. 3.2). Such

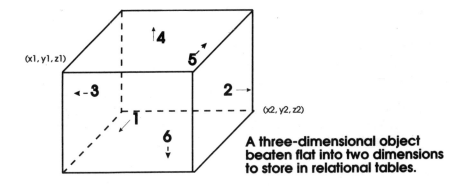

A three-dimensional object beaten flat into two dimensions to store in relational tables.

Object	Face
Sqr1	1
Sqr2	2
Sqr3	3
Sqr4	4
Sqr5	5
Sqr6	6

Face	Xa	ya	za	xb	yb	zb
1	x1	y1	z1	x2	y1	z2
2	x2	y1	z1	x2	y2	z2
3	x1	y1	z1	x1	y2	z2
4	x1	y1	z1	x2	y2	z1
5	x1	y2	z1	x2	y2	z2
6	x1	y1	z2	x2	y2	z2

Figure 3.2 n-dimensional data.

is the case in research environments where the goal is to design new systems. In these environments the design process is iterative, causing both the structure of the data (schema) and the structure of the program to evolve over time.

Smith and Zdonik emphasize the difference between the types of applications for which conventional databases are adequate and those for which they are inadequate:[2]

> Conventional database management systems have been successful at supporting data-intensive record-processing applications. Although these applications often require a large amount of code to produce many varied reports, the level of complexity as measured by the interactions between modules is relatively low. We believe that there exists a large class of applications for which relational database systems and other more conventionally-structured database systems are too limited. These applications are characterized as complex, large-scale, data-intensive programs. This class of applications needs a database model that is more expressive and flexible than the relational model. Furthermore, this class of applications needs database technology that is designed to facilitate programming-in-the-large, i.e. designing, constructing, and maintaining large, complex programs.

3.4   The Impedance Mismatch Problem

One of the main motivations for the development of OODBMSs and better programming environments is the impedance mismatch problem (see Fig. 3.3). This problem has been aptly described by Bancilhon et al.:[3]

> We do believe that the main bottleneck to the productivity of the application programmer is the impedance mismatch between the programming language and the query language. This impedance mismatch cannot be solved by redefining the database box (i.e. by changing the frontier between the programming language and the database system) but by mixing database technology and programming language technology to build a complete system which will have the functionalities of a DBMS and of a programming language.

Thus, there exists a need, in relational databases, to coordinate procedural languages with relational set-at-a-time behavior. There is also a need to modify applications each time the database schema changes.

3.5   The Problems with Embedding Query Statements in Programs

A number of relational database systems provide an interactive SQL-based interface to the database as well as an embedded SQL-based

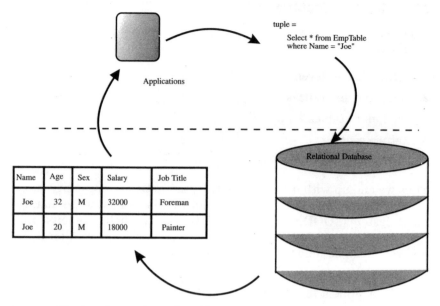

Figure 3.3 The impedance mismatch problem.

interface for an application programming interface. Embedded SQL interfaces provide a means to bridge the differences in syntax and semantics between the host programming language and the database language, namely SQL. There are five serious problems with embedding query statements in a general-purpose programming language:[4]

1. The data model of the database and the type system of the programming language do not match. For example, programming languages do not provide sets as a basic type, and sets of objects returned by a query cannot be manipulated directly by the programming language constructs.

2. Since there is no type system spanning the application and the query code, limited type checking can be done across the junction.

3. Queries can be formulated only on persistent data objects, and cannot be formulated against transient objects and persistent objects after they have entered the application address space.

4. Query and programming language statements cannot be freely combined.

5. The syntax and semantics of the two languages are completely different, and the programmer needs to learn to be aware of the differences.

3.6 SQL DBMS Problems

There are five areas where SQL DBMS differences can affect interoperability:

1. Syntactical differences
2. Semantic differences
3. Dictionary tables
4. Return codes
5. Host language interface

Thus we end up with different DBMSs, semantic heterogeneity, etc.

Some researchers have suggested object-oriented database management systems (OODBMSs) as a solution to the heterogeneity problem. By encapsulating data and the procedures to operate on it, the difference can be hidden from the user or application.

3.7 Data Models for Complex Objects

Database modeling paradigms can be compared along a number of dimensions:[5]

- Treatment of object identity
- Issues of redundant structure
- Notions of type and class
- Treatment of ISA relationships

Several modeling paradigms have been identified for complex objects:[5]

- Complex object types
- Semantic models
- Complex object models using object identifiers
- Models of certain conceptual languages

There are two different ways of modeling objects: providing direct representations of objects found in the real world, or just providing descriptions of those objects. This issue has ramifications for schema representation, user interactions, and data manipulation languages. The relational models use tuples or keys to represent object identities. The manipulation of data about entities is accomplished through manipulations of the values of the data that are used to represent them. In relational models, the values of specific attributes of objects are used for object identification, making them *value-based.* Semantic models, on the other hand, provide mechanisms for representing entities without employing their associated attributes and values for representation. Such semantic models are *object-based,* and there is always a one-to-one correspondence between abstract objects in the database and the real-world entities that they represent.

Complex object models are usually based on the theme of employing a small number of constructs, including *tuple* and *set,* to build hierarchical database structures. The nested relational model is perhaps the first such model found in the literature. The value-based nature of such complex object models burdens them with significant disadvantages in referencing data about entities.

The semantic models overcome some of the disadvantages of the complex object models by approaching object identity differently. For example, the object-based functional data model (FDM) schema employs abstract classes that contain objects, which correspond to concrete or conceptual entities in the real world. Abstract objects might be represented using internal identifiers or surrogates, but, in general, they are not directly accessible to database users.

The logical data model (LDM) in many respects follows the philosophy of complex object models, and also provides a form of object identity through the use of *l-values,* which are used in the construction of all structured objects. Both database models that have roots in programming languages and semantic data models have the ability to define essentially arbitrary data types for representing entities in the real world.

Object-oriented database models borrow concepts from both semantic models and the object-oriented paradigm of programming languages.

3.8 The Nested Relational Database Model (NRDM)

In this model, the database is defined as a set of nested relational structures. A component of a tuple in such a structure can be an atomic value or a nested relational structure. This type of nested structure contrasts with classical relational models, in which a database is defined as a set of flat relations or tables in which components of the tuple are always atomic values.

Deshpande and Van Gucht[6] have proposed the following operations on NRDM:

- Union
- Difference
- Project

- Select
- Join
- Nest
- Unnest

The nested algebra operations like select, join, and nest are value-driven, whereas project and unnest are not. Deshpande and Van Gucht have proposed two tightly coupled data structures, VALTREE and RECLIST, for efficient execution of updates and queries in the extended relational algebra of the NRDM. VALTREE is a structure for storing all the atomic values present in the tuples and sub-tuples of the database, and is suitable for performing value-driven operations. RECLIST is a record-list structure that is used for each structure in the NRDM.

3.9 Object-Oriented Database (OODB) Systems

OODBs are systems that can be used to store and retrieve objects and to provide facilities to manipulate stored objects. OODBs make it possible to store in a database a complete object as it exists in memory, without having to change the structure and representation of the object. It is possible to store and retrieve complex objects. This is perhaps the most important reason why OODBs have attracted the majority of users that have been dissatisfied with conventional database models.

One of the benefits of an OODB is the ability to build into the database knowledge about the data it contains, about data interrelationships, and about operations on the data. Objects can be related to other objects through inheritance, link, and embedded relationships. OODBs have the ability to maintain relationships between objects once these relationships have been established. Client applications accessing an OODBMS do not have to specify the relationships because they already exist in the database.

The strengths of OODBMSs can be summarized as follows:[1]

1. Suitability when data and relationships are irregular and complex
2. Tightly coupled, relatively transparent OOPL interfaces
3. Designed to take advantage of PC/workstation architectures, in terms of local memory and disk
4. Integration of non-DBMS data sources and applications

Loomis[7] has this to say about the advantages of harnessing OODBMSs: "Anyone interested in reusable code, decreased maintenance costs and better performance should be interested in OODBMS." Ingari is confidant that OODBMSs can help in distributed applications: "Corporations will eventually come to the realization that they cannot really move to a distributed computing environment without OODBMSs. Relational DBMSs simply are not well-suited to network computing."

3.10 Characteristics of Applications That Require OODBs

Clients of OODBs tend to have the following data characteristics:

- Complex data
- Evolutionary sets of data

The following are some examples of such systems. A more comprehensive list of such systems will be provided in a later chapter.

- Knowledge-based systems
- CAD/CAM design systems
- Program support environments
- CASE tools

If applications such as those used in genetic research have to model the complex data, an OODBMS would be the natural choice. Being able to create, store, and retrieve pictures of DNA molecules requires a database capable of storing images. While OODBMSs are capable of providing support for images, relational systems cannot support such applications.

Computer-aided design and computer-aided manufacturing (CAD/CAM) is another application area that is embracing OODBMS. Loomis[7] makes this observation: "In CAD/CAM, we are past the early adopter phase, and OODBMSs are a common accepted technology. CAD/CAM applications generate a lot of graphic information which creates problems with relational databases."

Mariani[8] has provided a good description of the characteristics of typical design systems (see Fig. 3.4):

- Objects are built from other objects, e.g., modules, submodules, books, chapters, sections, paragraphs, etc.
- The process is inherently iterative as the design evolves; conventional databases are "brittle" and do not cope with evolution easily.
- They need multiple levels of abstraction consisting of multiple components and need to be able to look into these components.

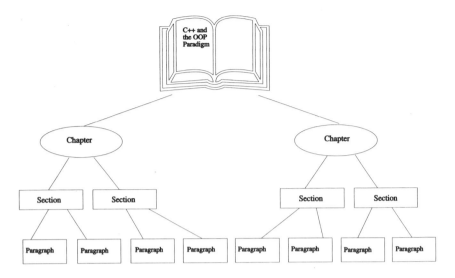

Figure 3.4 Complex data—a book or documents.

- The design task is shared among several designers. Designers will be modifying a certain part of the design and referring to the surrounding parts; there is a need to share component designs, and also to note that this sharing follows a certain pattern.

3.11   Potential Problems with OOP/OODBMS

There are several hurdles in the path leading to object orientation. Software development requires a methodology to facilitate the process. There are several nonstandard methodologies to choose from for object-oriented software development. The lack of a consensus on what OO methodologies should provide makes it difficult to come up with a standard in the industry. Each methodology delivers its own notation, strategies, activities, and guidelines.

Despite the hype by vendors, there are not enough robust tools in the market that support object-oriented software development. There are a wide array of tools available in the market for OO software development, most of them with insufficient market shares and questionable futures. Thus, OOT is being adopted by several corporations with high hopes for dramatic improvements, while the available software tools have not yet matured.

While relational databases and software tools that support relational data models are widely used in the industry, and are known to be robust and well designed, the same cannot be said of OODBMS and

OOP tools to date. Many commercial OODBMS suffer from the following problems:

1. Scalability.

2. Lack of support for industry standards.

3. Interworking between the object paradigm and other traditional approaches.

4. Lack of performance to support design and development of large-scale systems.

The OODBMS industry is likely to flourish with the development of complex database applications. Several OODBMS vendors have developed OODBMS products that facilitate the development of client-server architectures. The Object Management Group (OMG), an industry consortium, has addressed the standards issue, and has successfully developed standards for several pieces of vital technology that make distributed object-oriented software applications possible. Commercial applications are being built in several vertical markets with object-oriented databases. The market seems ripe for OODBMS technology and the OODBMS vendors are likely to develop more robust products to meet the challenge.

3.12 Migrating to an OOP/OODBMS Environment

As more application developers adopt object-oriented technology, several problems associated with migrating to a new software development paradigm surface, to the surprise and bewilderment of inexperienced developers. In order to make the migration manageable and less traumatic, it is important to address the technical and nontechnical problems that developers usually encounter. The first step is to identify why OOP is good for a project. Some valid reasons for opting for the OOP paradigm are (see Fig. 3.5):

1. Greater rigor and consistency in design

2. Reusability of design and software

Greater rigor and consistency in design
Reusability of design and software
Ease of maintenance
Ease of modifications

Figure 3.5 Reasons for employing OOT.

3. Benefits over the life cycle in terms of maintenance and modifications

The migration to a new paradigm is more likely to be successful if the people chosen to make the change have the right attitude toward the change. It is important to start the migration process with a team that has the necessary motivation to work with new technologies. It is also important to select OOP languages and tools that are appropriate to the project. This can only be ensured by a thorough evaluation of all tools and languages before selecting them for a project. One important issue to remember is that tool users have a tendency to become tool developers themselves, and thus sidetrack a project.

Scott Leibs'[9] observations about what trips up a migration to a client-server environment can also be applied to the migration to OOT.

1. Combining and coordinating products from multiple vendors, especially combining compilers and databases from vendors.

2. Changing the IS culture.

3. Immature applications development tools. This is particularly true with most OODBMS.

4. Training end users.

5. Moving down the OOP/OODBMS curve.

6. Network connections and reliability.

7. Integration and interoperability.

3.13 Easing the Trauma of the Paradigm Shift

Training is an essential component of a successful approach to any paradigm shift. Evaluating the training needs of a group of developers embarking on an OODBMS project is not easy or intuitive. Individuals who need to be trained usually do not know what they want. The trainers, therefore, must know more than their clients. One of the first skills that a beginner should acquire is a handle on OOP concepts, and one OOPL. Mike Banahan has analyzed the problem of migrating from C to C++, and has made some important observations:[1]

> The first significant effect is simply the length of time it takes to learn C++ well. Managers who are used to working with C programmers expect people to be able to learn C++ in about the same amount of time it takes to learn C, perhaps even a little less. After all, there are only a few new keywords and the biggest part of C++ is the ANSI C subset, isn't it? It takes a lot of patience before you can convince them that the facts of the matter are different. The second effect is that most of the skills of "traditional" procedural programmers are marginalized once you

migrate toward object-orientation. Now, I know that you can use C++ simply as a better C. But very few groups consciously have that as their objective; nearly all are aiming for OO at the end of the day. Every group ends up repeating the same experience and being surprised at the strangeness of the new territory.

Training is an ongoing issue with any new technology. A company's first set of applications with a new technology seldom takes full advantage of that technology. The problem generally faced by novices to OODBMSs is the tendency to write the first few applications as if the database were relational and not object-oriented. Continuing to design applications using a relational approach because of an inability to think in object-oriented terms is a significant roadblock to the adoption of an OODBMS. Breaking out of the relational mindset is what is required of new initiates to the OODBMS world.

Addressing the issue of problems faced with paradigm shifts, Taylor suggests,[10]

> The biggest danger for object technology is that people will dive into the new technology while holding onto their waterfall-style methodologies. In essence, when you have put together an object-centered model and built the classes to support it, you have a running business engine. The applications become just user interfaces to the engine, or special-purpose extensions to the engine.

There are essentially four modes of training:

1. Buy some books and give the staff the time to read them.
2. Choose "distance learning" techniques.
3. Use classroom-based training.
4. Use on-the-job training.

The importance of mastering OOP concepts, OOP languages, and OOP tools before embarking on a project cannot be underestimated. Several researchers have commented on the steep learning curve involved in mastering OOT. Objects provide a localized view of computing. It takes a whole group of cooperating components to provide the full functionality of the application. Each class in the application domain should do what it is supposed to. This cooperative quality of the object-oriented technology makes it ideal for distributed computing. Thus, new initiates to OOT have to appreciate the ramifications of an object-oriented approach. In addition to training developers in OOP concepts and OOPLs, it is imperative to provide good projects to practice the newly acquired skills. While the developers build up their expertise, they should be able to consult more experienced OO designers for technical know-how. *Object-oriented mentoring* is one good approach in which an experienced senior designer plays a mentoring role in the project by providing technical as well as managerial support to the junior members of the software development team.

The following migration-related issues have been identified by Archibald and Yakemovic:[11]

- Technology matters.

  - Make sure you are using the right criteria.
  - Focus on software engineering, not the language.
  - Don't mix technology creation with use.
  - Buy whatever you can.

- Management matters more.

  - Start small.
  - Pursue tangible goals.
  - Manage intensively.
  - Don't panic.

- OOP use is an investment—excessive ambition leads to unrealistic schedules.

- Training is essential.

One of the most difficult techniques to teach is the ability to reuse existing components. Software developers are used to cloning code, but not to reusing code. Cloning involves modifying borrowed code. All changes to the original code to improve its performance are unavailable to the clones. True reuse demands a significant discipline from the users.

To be able to use a class from a class library, the software developer should properly study the class library and understand the class hierarchies and the methods. This might take roughly half to one full day for each class. For a large class library with 300 or more classes, this might mean a long learning curve.[10]

Formal training in OOP and OOPLs is important. Trying to learn both OO concepts and an OOPL at the same time is neither easy nor effective. It is better to learn the OOP concepts well before attempting to learn an OOPL. This should be followed by some on-the-job training before any migration is attempted.

3.14   Object-Based Systems: Between Both Worlds

Object-based tools have gained in popularity in recent years in developing client-server applications. They are tools that support conventional environments while providing for the implementation of a part of their process or data models using objects. Such tools can also help integrate mainframes into the object-based, client-server environment. The main feature of object-based tools is the support for a conventional data model and a substantial portion of a conventional process model. They implement OOT in handling the user interface and can be considered to be object-oriented GUI front-end tools. The actual interface between the object environment and the conventional environment is handled in the messages of the objects. The methods of graphical objects tend to be procedural in nature and take the responsibility of mapping individual data items into an object.

Object-based tools provide an entry into the world of OO systems. They are considered easier to learn. Mitch Kramer[12] suggests that developers using object-based tools require two to three months to become proficient, compared to the four to six months required for OO.

3.15 Testing OO Software

Software testing has traditionally involved the following phases:

1. Unit tests of modules

2. Integration tests

3. System tests

After bugs in the software have been fixed, the software is subjected to regression tests to ensure correctness. These phases of software quality control are as important in OO systems as they were in traditional software development environments. However, one big difference in testing OO systems is the extra emphasis to be placed on completeness and correctness of software systems because of the reusability demands. It is not enough to ensure that the software works correctly; it is also important to ensure that the software can be reused in other settings, in applications other than the ones it was originally developed for.

The class is the building block for OO software. It is the unit of software development and must stand alone from the rest of the environment in which it is to be employed if it is to be truly reusable. Thus, while testing OO software, it is very important to test each and every class for completeness and correctness.

References

1. Jacob Stein, "Butter, Margarine, or Both? Muttered My Mother," *Journal of Object-Oriented Programming,* November–December 1992, pp. 20–21.
2. Karen Smith and Stanley B. Zdonik, "Intermedia: A Case Study of the Differences Between Relational and Object-Oriented Database Systems," *OOPSLA '87 Proceedings,* ACM, October 1987.

3. Francois Bancilhon et al., "The Design and Implementation of O2, an Object-Oriented Database System," *Lecture Notes in Computer Science, Advances in Object-Oriented Database Systems, 2nd International Workshop on Object-Oriented Database Systems,* Springer-Verlag, 1988.

4. Jose A. Blakeley, "DARPA Open Object-Oriented Database Preliminary Module Specification: Object Query Module," Texas Instruments Inc., Version 3, Nov. 25, 1991.

5. Richard Hull, "Four Views of Complex Objects: A Sophisticate's Introduction," in S. Abiteboul, P. C. Fischer, and H.-J. Schek (eds.), *Lecture Notes in Computer Science, 361, Nested Relations and Complex Objects in Databases,* Springer-Verlag, 1987.

6. Anand Deshpande and Dirk Van Gucht, "A Storage Structure for Nested Relational Databases," in S. Abiteboul, P. C. Fischer, and H.-J. Schek (eds.), *Lecture Notes in Computer Science, 361, Nested Relations and Complex Objects in Databases,* Springer-Verlag, 1987.

7. Paul Korzeniowski, "Object-Oriented DBMSs Strive to Differentiate," *Software Magazine,* May 1992.

8. John A. Mariani, "Object-Oriented Database Systems," in Gordon Blair, John Gallagher, David Hutchinson, and Doug Shepherd (eds.), *Object-Oriented Languages, Systems and Applications,* Halsted Press, 1990.

9. Scott Liebs, "Client-Server Report—Mastering the Migration Maze," *Information Week,* November 29, 1993, pp. 36–40.

10. Eric Aranow, "Object Technology Means Object-Oriented Thinking," *Software Magazine,* March 1992, 68–75.

11. Jerry L. Archibald and K. C. Burgess Yakemovic, "Panel: OOP in the Real World," Moderator Richard DeNatale, *OOPSLA/ECOOP '90, Addendum to the Proceedings,* ACM Press, 1990.

12. Mitch Kramer, "Developers Find Gains Outweigh OO Learning Curve," *Software Magazine,* Client/Server Computing Special Edition, November 1993, 23–33.

The Goals
of OODBMSs

Introduction

This chapter focuses on the debate on what constitutes an object-oriented database. While every database vendor in the industry would like to claim that its product does objects, end users are left with little clue as to how object-oriented the database really is. Researchers have addressed this very question of minimum set of requirements that can qualify a database as object-oriented. This chapter presents a brief description of their efforts.

4.1 The State-of-the-Art of OODBMSs

Object-oriented database management systems have received a lot of attention from both academia and industry in the last few years. Researchers have still not developed a strong data model that can characterize an OODBMS, and there is a lack of formal foundations for the field. A strong theoretical framework is necessary for future standardization of the technology. To promote the development of a common underlying model for all OODBMSs, several researchers joined forces to define OODBMS characteristics that such systems should possess. They have jointly proposed an "object-oriented database system manifesto" to be used as a straw man. The formal title for their document is "Third-Generation Data Base System Manifesto."[1] The manifesto proposes the following three basic tenets (see Fig. 4.1):

1. Besides traditional data management services, third-generation DBMSs will provide support for richer object structures and rules.

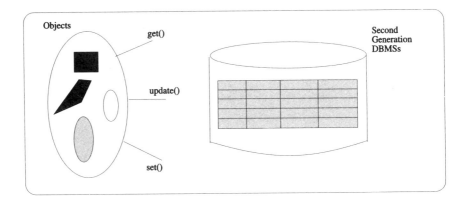

Third Generation DBMS: Subsumes Second Generation DBMSs
                          Supports Objects and Rules

Figure 4.1   Third generation DBMS subsumes second generation DBMS.

2. Third-generation DBMSs must subsume second-generation DBMSs.

3. Third-generation DBMSs must be open to other subsystems.

In addition to the tenets, the manifesto makes the following propositions:

1. A third-generation DBMS must have a rich type system.

2. Inheritance is a good idea.

3. Functions and encapsulation are a good idea.

4. Unique identifiers (UIDs) for records should be optionally assigned by the DBMS.

5. Rules will become a major feature in future systems. They should not be associated with a specific function or collection of records.

6. Navigation to desired data should be used only as a last resort.

7. There should be at least two implementations for sets of records, one using enumeration of members and one using the query language to specify membership.

8. Updatable views are essential.

9. Clustering, UID indexes, buffer pools in user space, etc., are physical rather than logical issues. To avoid compromising data independence, they must not show through to the user interface; therefore, they have nothing to do with the data model.

10. Third-generation DBMSs must be multilingual.

11. Persistent X for a variety of Xs is a good idea. They will all be supported on top of a single DBMS by compiler extensions and a complex run-time system.

12. For better or worse, SQL is intergalactic interspeak.

13. Queries and their resulting answers should be the lowest level of communication between a client and a server.

While proposing the OODBS manifesto, Atkinson et al.[2] separated the OODBS characteristics into the following three groups (see Fig. 4.2):

Mandatory: The ones the system must satisfy in order to be termed an object-oriented database system. These are complex objects, object identity, encapsulation, types or classes, inheritance, overriding combined with late binding, extensibility, computational completeness, persistence, secondary storage management, concurrency, recovery, and ad hoc query facility.

Optional: The ones that can be added to make the system better, but that are not mandatory. These are multiple inheritance, type checking and inferencing, distribution, design transactions, and versions.

Mandatory	
Complex objects	Extensibility
Object identity	Computational completeness
Encapsulation	Persistence
Classes	Secondary storage management
Inheritance	Concurrency
Overriding, late binding	Recovery
Ad hoc query facility	
Optional	
Multiple inheritance	Distribution
Type checking	Design transactions
Inferencing	Versions
Open	
Programming paradigm	Representation system
Type system	Uniformity

Figure 4.2 Proposed features for OODBMS.

Open: The points where the designer can make a number of choices. These are the programming paradigm, the representation system, the type system, and uniformity.

4.2 Requirements of Engineering DBMSs

Engineering applications require the DBMS to meet their unique demands on data, operations, environment, and performance. Most engineering applications have the following salient features:

Complex data: Data can be complex, and the relationships among data items can be multifarious.The ability to define, create, and modify arbitrarily complex data for engineering applications is very important. Data complexity can be in terms of cardinality of dimensions or the type of data. Bitmaps, three-dimensional geometric data, a stream of satellite data, etc., are examples of complex data. The size of such data can be a variable, possibly determined only at run time. The user must have the facilities to define new kinds of data as well as extend the functionalities of system-supplied data types.

Complex operations: The ability to define, create, modify, and delete data structures of any complexity implies that data should be modeled directly in terms of the application's entities and arbitrary operations on them. Thus engineering databases must support complex operations on individual instances of complex data as well as collections of such objects. The ability to create multiple (simultaneous) versions of components of complex data by means of linear and branch versioning is very important.

Distributed control in a heterogenous environment: In large engineering applications, there is often a need for heterogeneity and distribution of application components and data. Data distribution in a multiuser environment necessitates distributed concurrency control. The location of multiple databases in a distributed environment must be transparent to the application developers and the end users. Heterogenous environments require the DBMS to be available to a variety of applications running on workstations from different vendors.

High performance: Engineering DBMSs must meet the high-performance requirements of the various complex applications. Applications might need data from local databases or from remote databases. The required data must be presented without too much delay by the DBMS. The access to data should be as close as possible to in-memory data access.

4.3 Applications Using OOT and OODBMSs

Most engineering applications typically require flexible data modeling, complex data with complex relationships, large amounts of data, and high performance from hardware and software. Some applications are designed to be distributed across networks in a heterogenous environment. The choice of databases in such applications is very critical. In general, object-oriented databases are ideally suited for applications such as

1. Electronic computer-aided design (ECAD)

2. Mechanical computer-aided design (MCAD)

3. Computer-integrated manufacturing (CIM)

4. Computer-aided software engineering (CASE)

5. Computer-aided publishing (CAP)

6. Engineering designs, in general

7. Laboratory sciences

References

1. Malcolm Atkinson, Francois Bancilhon, David DeWitt, Klaus Dittrich, David Maier, and Stanley Zdonik, "The Object-Oriented Database System Manifesto," *Proceedings DOOD '89,* Kyoto, December 1989.
2. Malcolm Atkinson et al., "The Object-Oriented Database System Manifesto," in W. Kim, J. M. Nicols, and S. Nishio (eds.), *Deductive and Object-Oriented Databases,* North-Holland, New York, 1990.

OODB Features

Introduction

This chapter provides a detailed analysis of important features found in most object-oriented database systems (OODBs). Features such as transactions, concurrency control, versioning, and querying are presented in great detail. Object models recommended by DARPA's Open OODB project and OODBTG's Object Data Management model are also covered in this chapter.

5.1 Object-Oriented Database (OODB) Systems

The OODB paradigm is the combination of OOPL systems and persistent systems. The power of OODB comes from the seamless treatment of both persistent data, as found in databases, and transient data, as found in executing programs. The scope of the OODB paradigm includes[1]

- Programming model problems applied to the persistent data
- Database problems viewed in the context of a programming model

DARPA's Open Object-Oriented Database (Open OODB) project has proposed the following set of functional requirements for OODBs:

1. Object-oriented model, C++ or CLOS based
2. Persistence
3. Object translation
4. Concurrent access by multiple users

5. Distribution with location transparency

6. Query capability

7. Change management capability

8. Data dictionary

9. Class libraries

10. Integrity

11. Recovery

12. Security

13. Access to legacy data

14. User interface support

In this chapter, several of these features, along with a few others, will be discussed in detail.

5.2   Object-Oriented Data Model

The development of applications using OODBMS necessitates the use of object-oriented data models. The X3/SPARC/DBSSG/OODBTG ODB Reference Model proposes an abstract object model which several OODBMS vendors support. The Object Management Group (OMG) has also proposed an abstract object model for object-oriented applications. The details of the OMG's Object Management Architecture will be presented in a later chapter, and only a brief listing of important features of OMG's abstract object model is presented here.

The OMG abstract object model partially defines the model of computation seen by OMG-compliant applications. It addresses concepts related to object semantics and object implementation, and provides a generalized object model that is similar to those used in CLOS and Iris systems. The generalized object model is one where a client issues a request that identifies an operation and zero or more parameters, any of which may identify an object. Method selection may be based on multiple objects, and may be based on any of the objects identified in the request, as well as the operation.

A brief description of the OMG abstract object model is provided here:[2]

1. An object has an associated state and a set of operations.

2. Objects provide services to *clients*.

3. Clients request services by issuing *requests*.

4. Operations are identified by *operation names*.

5. Objects can be identified by their handles.

6. The behavior of a request for service generally depends on the actual parameters in the request and the state of the computational system.

7. Objects have identities. It should be possible to distinguish between objects and to compare two values to see if they identify the same object.

8. Each operation has an associated signature that may restrict the possible parameter values that are meaningful in requests that name that operation.

9. An *object type* is a type and the set of objects that satisfy the object type.

10. An *interface* to an object describes a set of potential requests in which an object can meaningfully participate. An *interface type* is defined by the set of objects that satisfy the particular interface by participating meaningfully in each potential request described by the interface.

12. Objects can be classified as *persistent* and *transient*.

13. Atomicity is a property of transaction systems which ensures that an operation either changes the state associated with all participating objects consistent with the request or changes none at all.

The OODB Task Group has proposed the following model for Object Data Management (ODM),[1] which includes the general characteristics of object models:

Object data management

General characteristics of object models

- Objects: operations, requests, messages, methods, state
- Binding and polymorphism
- Encapsulation
- Identity
- Types and classes
- Inheritance and delegation
- Noteworthy objects: relationships, attributes, literals, containment, aggregates
- Extensibility
- Integrity constraints
- Object language

Data management characteristics

- Persistence
- Concurrency and transactions
- Distribution
- ODM object languages and queries
- Data dictionary and namespace
- Change management: versions, configurations, dependencies, schema evolution
- Reliability and recovery
- Security

ODM system characteristics

- Class libraries
- Program and user interface
- User roles

The characteristics shown above are commonly shared characteristics of typical object data management systems.

5.3 Complex Objects

Complex objects, also referred to as *aggregate objects,* are formed by applying object constructors to simple objects such as integers and floats that are provided by all systems. The object space can be considered to be built on top of atomic objects of the types integers, floats, booleans, and strings.

A related term is *composition,* which is defined as the mechanism for forming a whole from component parts. Compositions have the advantage of reducing the complexity of design by treating a configuration of many things as one. Composition has been defined as a "consists of" association by some researchers. Many of the properties of the whole can apply to its parts as well. However, not all the properties of an object need to be inherited by or propagated to its components. Odell[3] has defined *immutable composition* as the act or result of forming an object that is immutably configured from its component parts. Each immutably composed object is created solely on the basis of its immutable component parts. Once created, an immutable object cannot change these components. Immutable components can be thought of as defining a composition because if another object were substituted, a different object would be defined.

Some important issues related to complex objects are

1. The storage structures used for complex objects
2. Query processing and execution strategies

3. Concurrency control and recovery algorithms for complex objects

4. Efficient execution strategies for the operators of the language

Other issues associated with complex objects are those of object equality and duplicate elimination.

5.4 Associations

Associations are constructs that logically link objects. *Composite objects* are logical objects that are made out of simpler objects by connecting them with associations.

Associations are useful in many situations. For example, a car manufacturer uses an object-based system to design two models of cars, the deluxe model and the luxury model. The two models have the same functional components—a car frame, a set of four wheels, an engine, gears, seats, and a steering wheel—but the actual components used for each model are of different quality and prices. The deluxe model uses a 4-cylinder engine, while the luxury model uses a 6-cylinder engine. The other components have similar differences.

Associations can be used to associate specific car components with a particular car model. As shown in Fig. 5.1, two car objects of class

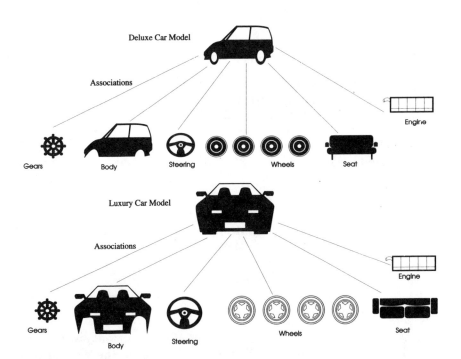

Figure 5.1 Association links for car parts.

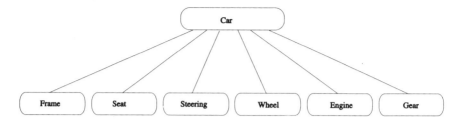

Figure 5.2   Association links between classes.

CAR are associated with objects of class FRAME, WHEEL, ENGINE, GEAR, SEAT, and STEERING wheel.

To create these associations, association links between the seven classes can be defined (Fig. 5.2). The following association links are necessary for class CAR:

- CAR to SEAT
- CAR to WHEEL
- CAR to GEAR
- CAR to FRAME
- CAR to ENGINE
- CAR to STEERING

5.5   Cardinality of Associations

The cardinality of associations is the number of objects involved on both sides of an association. In general, associations can be categorized into four groups according to their cardinality:

- $1:1$ = one-to-one
- $1m$ = one-to-many
- $m:1$ = many-to-one
- $n:m$ = many-to-many

The cardinality of an association is specified when the class is defined. In the car object, the relationship between the car and the wheel objects can be expressed by a one-to-many association. The CAR-to-FRAME association is one-to-one.

5.6   Persistence

Persistence requires that objects designated as persistent survive the process that created them. Persistence is based on the assumption that there is a pool of objects outside program scope that can be brought into a program and put back outside program scope when desired: such objects continue to exist after the program terminates.

The issue of what types can move between the application and the persistent object space is addressed differently by different OODBMSs. In some OODBMSs, some types that applications can manipulate cannot be made persistent, either because the semantics are not well defined or because there are practical limitations to translating certain types. In some systems, all object types can be represented in the persistent space.

5.7 Transactions

A *transaction* can be considered to be a sequence of operations being grouped together and treated as one indivisible logical unit. The grouped unit satisfies the ACID (Atomicity, Consistency, Isolation, and Durability) properties (see Fig. 5.3):

Atomicity: The effect is either total or none.

Consistency: The mapping is between consistent states.

Isolation: No information flows between active transactions.

Durability: The effect of commit is permanent in a database.

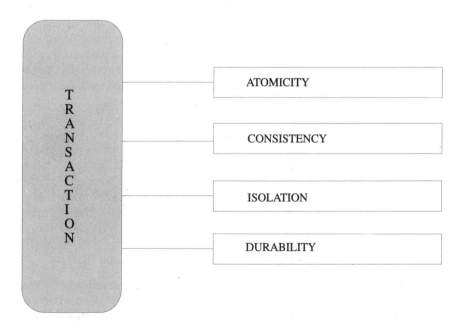

Figure 5.3 ACID properties of transactions.

One way of looking at transactions is to consider them a mechanism that allows applications to obtain permission to operate on certain objects in certain ways, subject to a set of concurrency control rules. In typical database applications, transactions are a proper vehicle to preserve consistency. A transaction is a sequence of database operations that transforms a consistent state of a database into another consistent state, without necessarily preserving consistency at all intermediate points. When a transaction terminates successfully, all the updates made within the transaction are persistent in the database. Transactions that fail do not update the database, and all changes made will be completely erased. The database system has to prevent concurrently executing transactions from seeing intermediate updates. Thus transactions are a

1. Unit of concurrency

2. Unit of recovery

The concept of transactions and the semantics of transactions tend to be application-specific, although traditional database systems tend to have a more rigid notion of a transaction around which the application programs are designed.

The commit operation is called to commit any changes made to shared objects to the global state of the database, making those changes available to other sessions. This operation also makes any changes by other sessions visible to the session executing the commit operation.

Transaction processing aims at solving the correctness problem, response time problem, and throughput problem associated with sharing data. These problems are orthogonal to other OODB problems such as persistence, query processing, and change management.

5.8 Long Transactions

When the objects being manipulated are large and complex, transactions may become much longer than their counterparts in typical database applications. Other transactions would have to wait for the objects to be released, and this wait could be a long one for large transactions. Conventional transaction models fall short of the requirements of long transactions involving complex data such as those found in engineering or design applications. Rehm et al. have described the issue of long transactions for design applications as follows:[4]

> We perceive a *design transaction* to comprise a unit of work not limited by the termination of an application program; it encloses an arbitrary series of checkout/checkin operations and maintains the consistency of the database involved. It enables the designer to manipulate one or more sharable objects in her/his own database without making them complete-

ly unaccessible for other designers. However, appropriate synchronization is provided to coordinate parallel activities. For instance, a designer is prevented from manipulating an object while another designer has checked it out for update. Design transactions are the kind of mechanism a database system should provide to support design processes.

Some OODBMSs model a long transaction as a series of short transactions.

5.9   Concurrent Access by Multiple Users

OODBMSs must be accessible by multiple users. When an application is accessing a section of the database, other applications must be permitted to access other sections of the database. Concurrency allows users to cooperate and collaborate in an application.

5.10   Concurrency Control

The concurrency control mechanisms are necessary to enforce serializability of ACID transactions. The basic modes of concurrency control are[1]

- Pessimistic mode
- Optimistic mode
- Mixed mode
- Semioptimistic mode

Pessimistic concurrency control avoids inconsistency by forcing a transaction to wait when there is a conflict and by releasing the transaction to proceed when the conflict is resolved. When a transaction is trying to commit, it does not introduce any inconsistency. Pessimistic concurrency control employs appropriate locking schemes, and two-phase locking is sufficient to ensure serializability in most cases.

The optimistic mode of concurrency control lets a transaction proceed as though conflict cannot occur and resolves inconsistencies that may have been introduced by performing a validation check at the time of commit. This is generally implemented using shadow copies of objects involved in the transactions and timestamps that are stored with each object. When committing a transaction, if the transaction's shadow copy remains valid (if the timestamp of an object in the shadow copy is younger than the one in the database), the transaction is committed. Otherwise, the transaction is aborted.

Mixed-mode concurrency control mechanisms are another option. *Intertransaction mixed-mode* and *intratransaction mixed-mode* mechanisms can be provided. In intertransaction mixed-mode, different transactions can use different concurrency control modes that coexist in one system. In intratransaction mixed-mode, a system employs different concurrency control modes for different data or data types within the same transaction.

The semioptimistic mode is another version of mixed-mode. A transaction in semioptimistic mode does not have to hold onto a lock until the transaction terminates as required by a strict two-phase locking protocol; a lock on an object can be released as soon as the use of the object is over or the modified object is saved in a database when updating an object.

There are several concurrency control algorithms that help ensure serializability. They include some based on[5]

1. Locking data items to prohibit conflicting accesses. Especially important is the two-phase locking technique, which guarantees serializability by requiring a transaction to obtain all the locks it will ever need before releasing any locks.

2. Timestamping accesses so the system can prevent violations of serializability.

3. Keeping multiple versions of data objects available.

5.11 Locks

Locks are needed in OODBs for several reasons:

- Concurrency control
- Synchronization

The following are the important types of locks commonly used in OODBMSs:[1]

Read locks: Used when a transaction reads an object and wishes to be guaranteed that no transaction can commit a newer version to the database while the lock is held. Several transactions can share a read lock.

Write locks: Used when a transaction needs to update the value of an object and make a new version of the object. Write locks are usually not shared with other transactions and are exclusive.

Null locks: Used when objects are not to be locked and when objects are managed in a cache outside a transaction. This is usually the value of locks after the transaction terminates.

Notify locks: Used for objects managed in a cache outside a transaction. Objects that are accessed using the notify locks cause the interruption of the program when a new value is committed in the database copy of the object. Thus, notify locks are used for objects that are kept in the cache even after the transaction has terminated.

Read locks and write locks are generally used inside a transaction boundary for concurrency control. Null locks and notify locks are used outside a transaction boundary for synchronization of objects.

5.12 Object Translation

OODBMSs can support multiple languages and multiple computational models. In the case of composite objects, where an object can have references to other objects, the interconnections can result in a graph whose closure may be very large. Ford et al. have addressed this issue in Zeitgeist,[6] and have identified the following two problems:

1. Translating the entire closure of an object pointer is very costly.

2. If an application (or applications) saves a pair of objects whose closures intersect, simply saving the two closures introduces a dangerous, hidden redundancy for data in the intersection of the two graphs.

The object translation service implies

1. Translation of objects in the client's computational form to the equivalent stored representation

2. Translation of a stored object into its computational form

5.13 Object Faults

An object faulting mechanism is employed by some OODBMS to move an object from persistent storage to the computational memory space. The object fault concept is similar to the concept of memory fault in virtual memory systems. There are several ways in which object faults can be implemented. One way is to trap references to reserved areas of memory.

Ford et al. have implemented an object faulting mechanism in Zeitgeist, and have described their scheme thus:[6] "The mechanism works by using a NULL-typed pointer to information identifying the object being referenced into a cell in memory. When a reference is made to that cell, an exception occurs that we can trap. At this point we materialize the object and allow the original reference to continue."

5.14 Pointer Swizzling

When virtual memory mechanisms are used to handle object faults, objects are always loaded into memory. In some OODBMSs, they are loaded in their entirety, while in others, only those pieces of an object that are actually needed are loaded into memory. In such an approach, the persistent storage layer is viewed as a persistent virtual memory. Each object pointer deference is preceded by a (software or hardware) check of the address format. If the pointer is in persistent identifier (PID) format, an object fault is signaled. The object is read into memory, giving it a valid local object number (LON) address, and the pointer which caused the fault is overwritten with that LON. This pointer translation is referred to as *pointer swizzling*. Once a pointer has been converted into LON format, it will no longer cause an object fault, although every reference is still subject to the run-time check.

Pointer swizzling approaches can be broadly categorized as

1. Strategies that use memory mapping techniques, similar to virtual memory

2. Strategies that employ software checks to detect accesses to non-resident objects

In the virtual memory approach, pages containing persistent data are allocated virtual memory addresses one step ahead of a program's actual usage of the pages. When a program accesses a page for the first time, a virtual memory page fault occurs, which is intercepted by the underlying object manager so that the page can be loaded into its preassigned location in memory.

Moss[7] has experimented with swizzling techniques based on software checks, and has recommended an object-at-a-time approach to swizzling in which objects that are in memory are classified as either swizzled or unswizzled objects. All pointers in an unswizzled object are swizzled immediately upon the first use of the object. After an unswizzled object has been accessed, it is marked as swizzled.

5.15   Version Control

Version management has been used to record the evolution of data. Modifications of data or code often introduce new bugs, and in such a case it is very important to know exactly what was changed. Historical version management can be used to "undo" unwanted modifications. In situations where a group of users is working on a set of objects at the same time, users often want to have their private workspace, in which they can modify objects without interference from others (see Fig. 5.4). Version management systems can help in managing and tracing these parallel developments.

The ability to create and maintain multiple versions of the same object is very important, especially in environments where the specifications of objects tend to change or evolve over time. This is a common phenomenon in design systems, where the designs are developed in an iterative process. Version control allows collaborating designers to

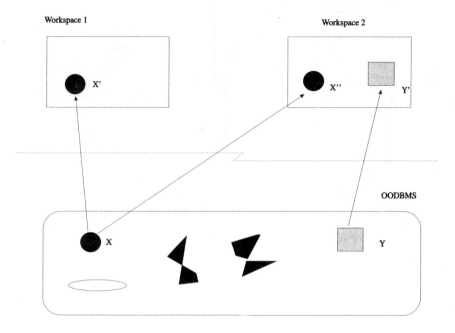

Figure 5.4 Checkin to workspaces from shared OODBMS.

express their different design concepts. Version control, however, does not include the facilities for merging contributions in a collaborative environment into a unified work. Merging requires other facilities.

There are some differences in how versioning is defined by OODBMS developers. One view is that objects are immutable with separate identity and that versioning is a predecessor/successor relation built on top of the OODB's notion of object identity. Another view is that versions are versions of the same object at different points, usually in time. The main issue is that of object identity.

One of the motivations for versioning is the necessity of maintaining enough historical data to reconstruct the complete state of the global object space as of an arbitrary point in the past.

Typical version update problems identified in the literature are

1. The indirect change problem
2. The multiple path problem

The indirect change problem occurs when a new version inherits a link to the previous version, and is thereby able to modify it. The multiple path problem results from simultaneous creation of a next version by two different nodes, thereby causing ambiguity as to which version should be accessed.[8]

5.16   Configuration Control

Combining components into a bigger construct, termed a *configuration,* requires a mechanism for selecting components according to a given criterion. A component must be allowed to be part of several different configurations.

Configuration management can be considered to be the management of the composition dimension of change management. Configuration management identifies how the managed objects, namely the configuration items, are composed from other managed objects. On some OODBMSs, configuration objects cannot be versioned.

It is possible, in some OODBMSs, to treat configurations as objects with state information. Such configuration objects are explicit configurations. Implicit configurations are also possible, in which some rule materializes configuration items.

Researchers working on the Open OODBM system at TI have identified a range of levels for the relationship between an object and its component:[9]

Versions: Specific versions of components are referenced, as needed in a released design.

Interfaces: The interfaces of objects are specified. Any object version which satisfies the interface requirements can be used. The common case is the object at time *t*, where *t* = now.

Contexts: A context is a sequence of change groups. This allows the designer to specify configuration object instances in terms of change groups.

Representations and / or host machines: Only the representations and/or host machines are specified. This is useful in specifying generic or representation-independent objects and distributed objects.

If the components of a configuration are bound to specific version objects, the configuration is referred to as *concrete.* If the components of a configuration are not bound to specific version objects, but are specified according to some user-specified characteristic, the configuration is called *generic, abstract,* or *dynamic.*

5.17   Checkin and Checkout to Private Databases

Typically engineering applications are run in a workgroup environment where work is collaborative in nature. The applications have a client/server architecture, with a public shared database on a database server and a private database on each client. Objects that are required for a specific task can be *checkedout* from the public database into the private database or workspace at the beginning of a transaction. At the end of a prolonged sequence of design operations spanning several design sessions, these objects are *checkedin* to the public database from which they were originally checkedout.

Objects are checkedout for read or update, and are appropriately locked in order to avoid any uncontrolled concurrency among parallel transactions. Such long-term transactions are very important in design environments, and provide cooperation in the sense that controlled sharing of intermediate results of long transactions is one of the fundamental means of cooperation.

Checkout/checkin mechanisms enhance the parallelism of activities. When objects are checkedout, their image in the original database will have to be locked from access by other transactions. There are several issues to be addressed by the checkin/checkout mechanism:

1. All object instances affected by a checkout operation have to be locked.

2. If multiple checkouts are allowed, the compatibility of the requested lock with an existing one has to be checked.

3. If some objects are shared by multiple complex objects, a designer may want to check out the composite object completely and thereby cause the locking of parts of a foreign object in the original database.

4. When objects are shared, the modification of the shared object after a checkin operation of its parent complex object might result in inadvertent modifications affecting all other objects that share the common object.

5.18 Schema·Evolution

As the number of applications that access a given class of objects grows, there is usually a need to modify the structure of the objects to better meet the needs of the applications. If the structure of a class of persistent objects is changed, all instances of that class are affected. The process of changing the structure or the behavior of persistent classes is usually referred to as *schema evolution*.

It should be possible to create, drop, rename, or change individual attributes and methods in the classes. Some OODBMSs permit such operations only on leaf classes in the hierarchy of classes. When attributes are dropped, it is not necessary to change all instances of a class or attribute to a null value in order to drop them.

Class specifications are usually altered by a designer in his or her own workspace. Class objects are then checkedin to the public section of the OODBMS. Changes made to the class objects need not be applied to all instances of the class. Changes can be applied to the objects as they are accessed during the normal course of events.

5.19 Data Dictionary

The data dictionary provides a repository for the information needed by other components of the OODB or user applications. Typically, the data dictionary is used to maintain information on data models/types, instances, names of instances, and applicable specific metadata. Some of the kinds of information maintained by a data dictionary are[10]

Data model and type information

- Type and class definitions
- Method or function signatures
- Representation of objects in different programming languages
- Physical representation of types in primary memory and secondary storage
- Specification of indices
- Class extents
- Data value integrity constraints
- Relationship constraints
- Mapping between objects in different data models

Instance information

- Cardinality of set instances
- Cost estimates and/or functions for accessing an instance
- Ordering of sets

Object naming information

- Mapping from a name to/from an object reference
- Collection of names into name contexts or directories

Application-specific information

- Specifications and design documents
- Module configuration and versioning

5.20 Distribution with Location Transparency

If the OODB supports distribution of objects, then it is important to provide transparency of location of the objects so that applications can be designed without having to incorporate mechanisms to locate objects. If the OODBMS application is to be scalable, it should be possible to move objects from one location (object server) to another to balance load. Objects at one location (on one server) must be able to refer to those at other locations (servers) in spite of object migrations.

The behavioral extension of the distribution of event execution is implemented by hiding the distinction between address spaces, thus giving the illusion of a large, flat address space. There are several strategies to give the illusion of a large, flat address space; one of them involves moving the object to the current execution space and then executing the event locally, and another involves executing the event remotely.

There are several ways to name objects in distributed environments. There are essentially two choices for object names: they can be location-independent or location-dependent. Location-independent names are referred to as *object identifiers* (OIDs). They have the advantage of being the same even when an object moves. Unfortunately, they tend to be large, sometimes as large as 40 bits. It is difficult to reuse object identifiers when objects are deleted. The large number of bits constituting the object identifiers can be structured in such a way that different object servers or databases can be made in charge of different parts of the object name space. Some OODBMSs employ 64 bits for the object identifiers. Applications can access objects by using the object identifiers, which can then be mapped from OIDs to object locations.

In general, there are several issues related to database distribution that need some attention when analyzing the technology. These issues are really problem areas:

1. Media failures
2. Large amounts of data
3. Machine failures
4. Networking partitioning
5. Physical movement of data
6. Integration of data from multiple databases
7. Wide-area networks (WANs)

To address the problems of media failure, machine failure, network partitioning, and WANs, multiple copies of data can be maintained. Replication of data can help solve the problem of moving large amounts of data across the network.

Distribution is not really a problem—it is a solution to the database problems of managing large amounts of data and providing high availability. Distribution and replication of a single logical database are sufficient to address the database problems listed above.

5.21 Query Capability

It should be possible to query simple objects as well as complex objects. It should also be possible, in an OODB, to query a collection of objects to retrieve the required object. When composite objects are used, it must be possible to navigate from one object to another using links representing associations between objects.

Object query languages have been approached in two ways:

1. SQL extensions
2. Extensions to an OO programming language

SQL is a database language that is declarative in nature. A declarative query language is a language in which a programmer can express what data to retrieve from the database without having to describe exactly how to efficiently retrieve them. SQL extensions in relational databases were the reason for the impedance mismatch problem. However, it would be easier to create an object-based SQL as a standard, thus making the query language language-independent.

Extending OOPLs to perform queries has the great advantage of using the same syntax as the programming language and thus avoiding the impedance mismatch problem. A major disadvantage is the difficulty of creating a standard for language extensions for querying. It is hard enough to create standards for one language; the coordination required for standardization of queries in multiple languages is almost insurmountable.

The DARPA Open OODB project at TI has proposed the following features as essential features of the underlying data model[11] that help determine the objectness of the object query language:

1. *Object identity,* that is, the ability of the system to distinguish between two different objects that have the same state. The state of an object can be shared by several objects via object identity.

2. *Encapsulation,* a kind of abstraction that enforces a clean separation between the external interface (behavior) of an object and its internal implementation. Encapsulation requires that all access (or interaction) with objects be done by invoking the services provided by their external interface.

3. *Complex state,* the ability to define data types whose implementation has a nested structure. The state of an object could be built from records of primitive types, other objects, or sets of objects.

4. *Type extensibility,* the ability to define new data types from previously defined types by enhancing or changing the structure or behavior of the types. Type inheritance is a mechanism used to define new types by enhancing already existing behavior.

5. *Genericity*. The types of the object data model with which the object query language collaborates must be generic. That is, as a new type is added to the system, it must be queriable.

5.22 Integrity

Referential integrity in relational databases was a kind of integrity constraint that guaranteed the existence of all objects referenced. In relation tables, foreign keys used to refer to tuples in other tables and referential integrity constraints guaranteed the existence of the referenced tuples. Similar integrity constraints are necessary in OODBMSs to ensure that the pointers to objects refer to actual objects.

5.23 Recovery

Recovery refers to the process of enforcing consistency after a transaction has aborted as a result of the state of certain objects, hardware failures, or communication problems. System failures, either of hardware or of software, should not result in inconsistent database states. Recovery is the technique used to provide this assurance. Recovery may be required to be total, with rollback in the event of unrecoverable loss, or partial recoverability may be allowed in some circumstances.

5.24 Security

Security is as much a concern in OO environments as it is in any other environment. Security mechanisms are necessary to protect operations and objects from illegal or dangerous actions. Access control mechanisms are typically employed to restrict access to objects or operations by other objects, systems, or users. Objects, users, and systems can be provided with certain capabilities that authorize them to perform certain operations.

Encryption and decryption techniques may be employed in OODBMSs to ensure security. Such mechanisms are useful in ensuring security during object migrations.

5.25 Access to Legacy Data

When existing database applications are redesigned and retooled using OOT and OODBMS, all preexisting data must still be accessible from the new environment. Such data are termed *legacy data*. One option is to migrate the legacy data to the new environment. This may not be easy, and it usually takes a lot of time and expense to migrate all the data. Another option is to keep old legacy data in their own environment, and provide connectivity to the old system. The development of OODB interfaces to legacy database systems to permit data access from new OO applications is a good option. However, the users can end up supporting two environments instead of one.

5.26 User-Interface Support

With an ever-increasing number of user-interface component libraries to choose from, it takes relatively little work to integrate them into OODBMS applications. Several OODBMS products come bundled with vendor-supplied user-interface libraries. With some care, the application developer should be able to incorporate the features from other user-interface component libraries with those suppled by the OODBMS vendor.

The Smalltalk-80 programming environment provided a good user-interface architecture called the Model-View-Controller (MVC). Several other OO systems have adopted MVC as a basis for user-interface design. The *model* is the component that provides an interface to the application. The *view* is the component used to display some aspect of a particular application. The information displayed by the view is obtained by requesting current state information from the model. The *controller* is used to interpret user input actions that result in changes to the state of the application via the model.

Most window managers have borrowed some of the features of the MVC mechanism. The X11 user-interface system provides user-selectable window managers and the ability to connect to client programs on the same or different machines.

The ObjectStore OODBMS from Object Design Inc. supports the Motif GUI on UNIX environments and the Windows GUI on personal computers with Microsoft Windows. Other OODBMS products also provide similar GUI support on both the UNIX and the Microsoft Windows environments. However, there is no easy connectivity between applications developed on rapid application development platforms such as Powersoft's Power Builder or Enfin, and the commercially available OODBMS. In the near future, OODBMS vendors will have to address the issue of providing connectivity to application front-ends developed using GUI based rapid-application development environments.

References

1. Chung C. Wang, "DARPA Open Object-Oriented Database Preliminary Module Specification: Extended Transactions," Texas Instruments Inc., Version 2, Nov. 25, 1991.
2. Object Management Group, *OMA Guide,* 1992.
3. James Odell, "Managing Object Complexity, Part II: Composition," *Journal of Object-Oriented Programming,* vol. 5, no. 6, 1992, pp. 17–20.

4. S. Rehm et al., "Support for Design Processes in a Structurally Object-Oriented Database System," *Lecture Notes in Computer Science, Advances in Object-Oriented Database Systems, 2nd International Workshop on Object-Oriented Database Systems,* Springer-Verlag, 1988.

5. Avi Silberschatz, Michael Stonebraker, and Jeff Ullman, "Database Systems: Achievements and Opportunities," *Communications of the ACM,* vol. 34, no. 10, 1991, pp. 110–120.

6. Steve Ford et al., "ZEITGEIST: Database Support for Object-Oriented Programming," *Lecture Notes in Computer Science, Advances in Object-Oriented Database Systems, 2nd International Workshop on Object-Oriented Database Systems,* Springer-Verlag, 1988.

7. J. Eliot B. Moss, "Working with Persistent Objects: To Swizzle or Not to Swizzle," COINS Technical Report, May 1990.

8. Kotcherlakota V. Bapa Rao, Anat Gafni, and Georg Raeder, "The Design of Dynamo: A General-Purpose Information Processing Model with a Time Dimension," *Lecture Notes in Computer Science, Advances in Object-Oriented Database Systems, 2nd International Workshop on Object-Oriented Database Systems,* Springer-Verlag, 1988.

9. Craig Thompson, "DARPA Open Object-Oriented Database Preliminary Module Specification: Change Management Module," Texas Instruments Inc., Version 2, Nov. 25, 1991.

10. Edward R. Perez, "DARPA Open Object-Oriented Database Preliminary Module Specification: Data Dictionary," Texas Instruments Inc., Version 3, Nov. 20, 1991.

11. Jose A. Blakeley, "DARPA Open Object-Oriented Database Preliminary Module Specification: Object Query Module," Texas Instruments Inc., Version 3, Nov. 25, 1991.

6

Persistence

Introduction

This chapter addresses the issue of persistence in great detail. Persistence is not a new idea. All databases provide persistence. The issue of accessing data in a program at run time from persistent storage rather than from volatile memory has been the focus of object-oriented database research for several years. In this chapter, the issues of persistence as it relates to type and security are explored in detail.

6.1 The Lifetime of Data

The lifetime of data in a program can be different for different kinds of data. Local variables in a procedure are usually considered automatic and exist only when the procedure is activated. While computing results of expressions, the intermediate results are usually transient in nature and don't need any variables. Data that are saved in memory created using the `malloc()` functions, or memory allocated from heap, live longer than automatic variables unless they are explicitly returned to heap. The scope of global variables gives them more visibility, and they live longer than automatic variables in a procedure. Some data outlive the program. Between different executions of the same program, some data can be saved in files or databases.

Data in a programming language can be independent of their lifetime. It is possible to abstract out the persistence property of data. This makes it possible to view data in programming languages just as they are viewed in databases. Languages that support persistence of data can also be used as database programming languages.

6.2 Persistence

Persistence is a property of objects. An object is called persistent if its lifetime is independent of the lifetime of the creating program. Traditionally, files and database records have been the only mechanisms providing persistence. Persistence has also been defined as the ability of types (or methods or objects) to "survive" the execution of the module (the program or method in our system) in which these types (or instances) are defined and created. This persistence mechanism is considered to be one of the main characteristics of database programming languages. Bancilhon et. al.[1] have identified the following two distinct aspects of persistence (Fig. 6.1):

1. The type is not destroyed when the program or method in which it is defined terminates.
2. The type is associated to a global name by which it can be referenced throughout the system.

The first of these aspects of persistence deals with the internal garbage collection of types, while the second one deals with the scope of the type definition.

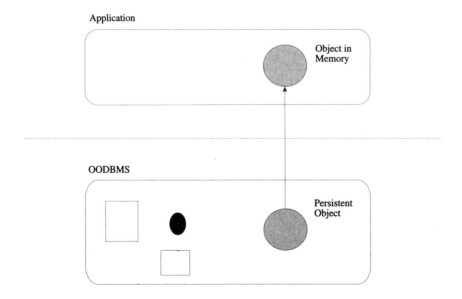

Figure 6.1 Persistence.

6.3 Security

Typically, a system is considered secure if it provides[2]

- *Integrity:* Data or programs are not changed accidentally or on purpose without the necessary authority.

- *Confidentiality:* Data are not made available inappropriately or without the necessary permissions.

- *Dependability:* To rightful users, the system functions are available as specified.

6.4 Security and Persistence of Objects

The most natural and attractive protection mechanism for object-oriented systems is *capability-based addressing.* A capability is informally equivalent to a ticket in the sense that possession of the ticket allows the holder of the ticket access to the object described in the capability, provided that the access mode is compatible with the access rights stored in the capability.[3]

In the MONADS-PC system, capabilities have the following properties:

- Each capability contains a virtual address used to identify the object to which it provides access.

- Identifiers (virtual addresses) are unique and are never reused to refer to a different object.

- Each capability also contains a list of operations which its holder may invoke on the object.

- There may be several capabilities for an object, possibly with different access rights, allowing several users to have shared access to an object.

- There is no way of forging a capability or changing its contents in an unauthorized way.

In the BiiN[2] architecture, the system's addressing was centered around a capability mechanism and a tagged memory architecture. Each memory word was 32 bits long, with an additional tag bit that was used to identify capability. The 33-bit memory word with the tag bit "on" was called an *access descriptor* (AD). Each access descriptor of 32 bits had the following components:

- An *object index* that identified an entry in the *object table:* The object table entry contained an AD to the type identifier of the object and the base address of the page table where the object's memory pages were administered.

- *Type rights:* The object comes with three generic type rights (use, modify, control).

- *Representation rights:* The read and write representation rights are checked at each access to a page of the object the AD points to.

In BiiN, the system could distinguish between active and passive objects. An active space contained only active objects. Passive space comprised all passivated objects. Persistent storage support involved transparently mapping the active space representation of objects to their passive representation, and vice versa.

6.5 Principles of Orthogonal Persistence

Several researchers have studied the relationships between persistence of data and other attributes of data, and have identified the following principles which define the persistent abstraction:[4]

- *The principle of persistence independence:* The persistence of data is independent of how the program manipulates the data. The system takes care of moving the data between secondary storage and the main memory. The user does not have to control such data movements.

- *The principle of data type orthogonality:* All types of data allowed by the programming language should be permitted the entire range of persistence; i.e., persistence should not be restricted to a subset of the allowable types of data.

- *The principle of persistence identification:* The choice of the identification system used to provide object identification and the mechanism for providing persistence is orthogonal to (independent of) the universe of discourse of the system. This means that the mechanism employed to identify persistent objects is not influenced by, and has no influence on, the type system.

Morrison and Atkinson claim that the application of these three principles yields *orthogonal persistence*. They also suggest that the savings of persistent systems is in reduced complexity for application builders:

> Traditionally the programmer has to maintain three mappings among the database model, the programming language model, and the real world model of the application. The intellectual effort in maintaining the mappings distracts the programmer from mastering the inherent complexity of the application to concentrate on overcoming the complexity of the sup-

port system. In a persistent system, the number of mappings is reduced from three to one, thereby simplifying the application builder's task.

Some of the other advantages of persistence include protection mechanisms that operate over the whole environment, referential integrity, and reduced code size as a result of the persistent features that implement long-term preservation and restoration of data.

6.6   Costs of Providing Persistence

Persistence can be provided only if there exists a stable object store, a mechanism for storing objects so that they can be efficiently retrieved. Clustering of persistent objects on secondary storage is a common phenomenon. Associate retrieval is another feature that is frequently employed to speed queries of persistent objects in most object-oriented databases.

References

1. Francois Bancilhon et al., "The Design and Implementation of O_2, an Object-Oriented Database System," *Lecture Notes in Computer Science, Advances in Object-Oriented Database Systems, 2nd International Workshop on Object-Oriented Database Systems,* Springer-Verlag, 1988.
2. M. Reitenspieb, "An Architecture Supporting Security and Persistent Object Storage," *Security and Persistence,* Bremen 1990, Workshops in Computing, series edited by Professor C. J. van Rijsbergen, Springer-Verlag.
3. B. Freisleben and P. Kammerer, "Capabilities and Encryption: The Ultimate Defense against Security Attacks?" *Security and Persistence,* Bremen 1990, Workshops in Computing, series edited by Professor C. J. van Rijsbergen, Springer-Verlag.
4. R. Morrison and M. P. Atkinson, "Persistent Languages and Architectures," *Security and Persistence,* Bremen 1990, Workshops in Computing, J. Rosenberg and J. L. Keedy (eds.).

7

Object Identity

Introduction

This chapter addresses the issue of object identity. The differences in the concept of object identity in relational systems and in object-oriented systems are highlighted. The problems with value-based identity are enumerated, and the advantages and disadvantages of an object-based approach are described briefly.

7.1   Object Dynamics

In an object-oriented system, objects are organized into object types, within a sophisticated subtyping mechanism. Objects need to be created and perhaps initialized before they can be used. Objects may be changed and manipulated in several different ways. Finally, they may be destroyed.

7.2   Identity in Programming Languages

Traditional programming languages support identity by means of user-defined names. Variables and filenames are examples of identity. The actual binding of an object to its name occurs at run time in most cases. Thus, addressability and identity are merged in programming languages, although they are different concepts.

There is a great difference between addressability and identity. Addressability provides a means to access the object. It is a feature external to the object. Its implementation is dependent on the environment. Object identity is internal to the object. It is a means of representing the individuality of an object independent of how it is to be accessed. Khoshafian and Copeland[1] explain,

There are practical limitations to the use of variable names without some built-in representation of identity and operators to test and manipulate this representation at an abstract level. One problem is that a single object may be accessed in different ways and bound to different variables without having a way to find out if they refer to the same object.

7.3 Data Identity in Relational Databases

In the relational approach, the data associated with an object are stored as a tuple in a table. One or more attribute values are used to actually identify each object stored in a relation. Thus the actual value(s) of object attributes are used as object identifiers. Often, several attribute values, making up a significant portion of the object's structure, are employed to identify an object, when a simple key is not sufficient. There is no mechanism in the relational model for representing entities in a manner essentially independent of their associated attributes and values. Thus, users and designers are forced to think of objects in terms of their values while using the relational model, and there is no other way to access objects. Moreover, relationships between different objects are represented only in terms of relationships of their associated values.

User-defined identifier keys can be used in relational systems to provide object data identity. SQL and Prolog are languages where the identifier keys are formed by some subset of the attributes of the object. In such cases the concepts of data values and identity are mixed.

There are several repercussions of employing attribute values as part of the object's identification. If an attribute value changes, does the object change its identity? A changed attribute value may introduce ambiguity in interpretation, as it may suggest a change in the state of an object as well as the creation of a new entity. Often, identifier keys are not allowed to change despite the fact that they are user-defined. If the set of attributes used as identifier keys is changed, it may result in a discontinuity in identity of some of the data objects.

7.4 The Need for Object Identity

The identity property of an object helps distinguish it from all other objects in the system. Object identity should be independent of object content, its location, and its addressability. Object identity must provide for object sharing. Object types can be determined by a coherent identification system where object instances can be associated with specific identifiers.

In OO environments, object identification can be provided independent of attribute values, unlike in relational database environments.

Identification by addressability, as in programming languages, is another mechanism that compromises identity. Object identification can be provided by means of *surrogates* and *naming operations*. Some identification mechanisms[2] adopt the viewpoint that *an identification system is an algebraic data type.*

Object models incorporating object identity can be defined with appropriate operators that manipulate object identity. Khoshafian and Copeland[1] define an object system as a set of objects. It is consistent if

1. No two distinct objects have the same identifier (unique identifier assumption). In other words, the identifier functionality determines the type and value of the object.

2. For each identifier present in the system, there is an object with this identifier (no dangling identifier assumption).

Such a definition of a consistent object system allows for objects becoming members of multiple sets without the need for replicating objects. An object is permitted to become a member of several other objects. It also allows for attribute assignments without replications.

Stemple et al.[3] have proposed assignment of system-supplied, immutable identifiers for each object, such that

1. Every object has a unique identifier, i.e., an object identifier functionally determines the object's type and value.

2. For every identifier present in the system, there exists an object with this identifier, i.e., no dangling references are allowed.

Such a strong sense of object identity allows objects to be shared, and associations among entities can be modeled by relating the corresponding objects and not external references, such as user-defined attributes.

Paton and Gray have provided the following definitions for object identity:[4]

1. An object has an existence and an identity which is independent of its value.

2. Identity is that property of an object which distinguishes the object from all others.

An object ID can be considered to be a surrogate for the object. It is not the actual address in memory. It is an indirection to locate the object. In most OODBMSs, the object ID, as a surrogate, contains an indication of whether the object instance is volatile, persistent, or deleted. When an object is referenced, the object ID introduces an indirection, which is a disadvantage. However, surrogates have several advantages—they enable objects to be switched between volatile and persistent states.

7.5 Problems with Employing Value-Based Representation of Objects

1. It forces users to think in terms of values when trying to manipulate objects.
2. Objects cannot be referenced directly.
3. Relationships between objects can be represented only through relationships of their associated values.
4. Combinations of attribute values have to be employed for object identification if simple keys are not available.
5. Ambiguities concerning the update of values: does the resulting value refer to a new entity, or does it just reflect a change in the data value of an existing entity?

7.6 Problems with Object-Based Approach

1. It is often difficult to obtain a specific object without navigating.
2. Associative access of required objects is through some related object or value. Some syntactic sugar is necessary to make it user-friendly.

7.7 Operators for Objects with Identity

It is often useful to identify whether two objects are identical. An operator can be designed to test whether two objects are the same. It is also very useful to test two objects for equality. Equality tests can be of two types:

1. Shallow equality
2. Deep equality

Two objects are *shallow-equal* if their values are identical, i.e., if all scalar attributes of the object have the same value and all subobjects are identical. *Deep equality*[1] is defined as follows:

1. Two atomic objects are deep-equal if their values are the same.
2. Two set objects are deep-equal if they have the same cardinality and the elements in their values are pairwise deep-equal.

3. Two tuple objects are deep-equal if the values they take on the same attributes are deep-equal.

In short, two objects are deep-equal if all scalar attributes have the same value and all subobjects are deep-equal.

It is also useful to define update operators for set objects and tuple objects. For tuple objects, an assignment operator can be defined to assign an object to an attribute of the tuple. For set objects, operators can be defined to add an element to a set and to remove an element from a set.

In some situations, it might be necessary to merge two objects and make them a single object. Thus a merge operator might also be necessary in object systems.

References

1. Setrag N. Khoshafian and George P. Copeland, "Object Identity," *OOPSLA '86 Proceedings*, September 1986, pp. 406–415.
2. H. D. Ehrich, A. Sernadas, and C. Sernadas, "Abstract Object Types for Databases," *Lecture Notes in Computer Science, Advances in Object-Oriented Database Systems, 2nd International Workshop on Object-Oriented Database Systems*, Springer-Verlag, 1988.
3. David Stemple, Adolfo Socoro, and Tim Sheard, "Formalizing Objects for Database using ADABTPL," *Lecture Notes in Computer Science, Advances in Object-Oriented Database Systems, 2nd International Workshop on Object-Oriented Database Systems*, Springer-Verlag, 1988.
4. Norman W. Paton and Peter M. Gray, "Identification of Database Objects by Key," *Lecture Notes in Computer Science, Advances in Object-Oriented Database Systems, 2nd International Workshop on Object-Oriented Database Systems*, Springer-Verlag, 1988.

8

OODB Architectures

Introduction

This chapter is designed to provide a brief introduction to the architecture of object-oriented database management systems. It provides a description of some of the research issues involved in the design of such systems.

8.1   User Demands of OODBs

Researchers at TI working on the Zeitgeist project conducted interviews with application developers who were potential users of OODBs, as well as programmers responsible for maintaining existing code, and identified five important user demands:[1]

1. Application developers and maintainers were not interested in an OODB that would require them to write their applications in a different programming language or use a data model different from the one offered by their programming language.

2. Application developers and maintainers would not use an OODB that restricted their use of language constructs for objects stored in the database or required them to explicitly translate their objects into a form the database could handle.

3. Application developers and maintainers strongly preferred that operations involving persistent objects be distinguishable from operations on nonpersistent objects.

4. When presented with the option, application developers and maintainers preferred a database interaction model that did not require explicit fetches of objects before they could be manipulated.

5. Application developers, maintainers, and their managers preferred a database able to operate in a world of distributed computers using a variety of architectures.

8.2 OODB Architectures

McLeod[2] has attempted to characterize an OODB precisely by placing it in contradistinction to a record-oriented database:

Individual object identity: Abstract objects can be directly represented and manipulated in a database, independent of symbolic surrogates for them. Objects at various levels of abstraction and of various modalities can be accommodated.

Explicit semantic primitives: Primitives are provided to support object classification, structuring, and data integrity. These primitive abstraction mechanisms, supporting such features as aggregation, classification, instantiation, and inheritance, have their roots in "semantic data models" and artificial intelligence knowledge representation techniques.

Active objects: Database objects can be active as well as passive, in the sense that they can exhibit behavior. Various specific approaches to the modeling of object behavior can be adopted, such as an interobject message-passing paradigm. The important point is that procedures to manipulate data are represented in the database itself.

Object uniformity: All information in a database is described using the same object model. Thus, descriptive information about objects, referred to here as meta-data, is conceptually represented in the same way as specific "fact" objects.

8.3 Architecture of the O_2 System

The O_2 OODB system was developed by INRIA to provide a complete application development environment that would include those of a DBMS, those of a programming language, and those of a programming environment. The O_2 system consists of four modules:[3]

- Data manager
- Method manager
- Type manager
- Precompiler

The *data manager* creates, stores, and maintains objects. The *type manager* creates, stores, and maintains type structure descriptions; it corresponds to the notion of a schema manager in a classical database system. It also manages the description of methods of the application program objects. The *method manager* creates, stores, and maintains source and object code of methods. The *precompiler* takes as input CO_2 programs, calls the type and method managers to perform type checking, and generates C programs with calls to the data and method managers.

The data manager is made up of three layers. The innermost layer is responsible for communicating with the server machine. The intermediate layer deals with the memory hierarchy. It implements an object virtual memory mechanism. The outermost layer is made up of primitives that provide the following support:[2]

1. Message passing to an object

2. Predefined method implementation

3. Object creation and deletion

4. Transaction management primitives connecting to those provided by the underlying file system

8.4 The Zeitgeist Architecture

The Zeitgeist architecture was based upon the goal of providing seamless integration of database and programming environments and the provision of orthogonal persistence. The Zeitgeist architecture builds the capabilities of persistent objects in the same way the capabilities of objects are built in OOPLs. The architecture consists of three components:[1]

1. Persistent object store (POS)

2. Object management system (OMS)

3. Set-oriented interface

At the lowest level of Zeitgeist, the POS, where unencapsulated data structures are manipulated, the passive object paradigm is supported. Class definitions, object instances, methods, and functions are all passive at this level, and are also supported. The OMS implements the active object paradigm, where programs interact with the database by sending messages to encapsulated objects held by the database. Messages are sent to surrogates for encapsulated persistent objects, and the corresponding objects are materialized by OMS using the POS capabilities. The set-oriented interface provides set-oriented capabilities that can be used to manipulate encapsulated objects. This layer provides for querying facilities.

8.5   The ObjectStore Architecture

ObjectStore is a popular OODBMS that is widely used in engineering environments. It provides DBMS functionality distributed over a network using a client/server model.

The main features of the ObjectStore architecture are

1. Virtual memory mapping
2. Caching to minimize disk and network overhead
3. Support for client/server architecture

The salient features of the ObjectStore process architecture are

1. ObjectStore employs a client/server paradigm.
2. ObjectStore Server manages data on behalf of client applications.
3. Each Server manages a database stored in files or raw partitions.
4. The Directory Manager is responsible for mapping hierarchical database names to Servers.
5. The database is arranged in a directory hierarchy that resembles the file systems in UNIX.
6. A Cache Manager is used on client machines.

ObjectStore supports nested transactions to any arbitrary depth. It does not support shared and grouped transactions.

References

1. Steve Ford et al., "ZEITGEIST: Database Support for Object-Oriented Programming," *Lecture Notes in Computer Science, Advances in Object-Oriented Database Systems, 2nd International Workshop on Object-Oriented Database Systems,* Springer-Verlag, 1988.
2. Dennis McLeod, "A Learning Based Approach to Meta-Data Evolution in an Object-Oriented Database," *Lecture Notes in Computer Science, Advances in Object-Oriented Database Systems, 2nd International Workshop on Object-Oriented Database Systems,* Springer-Verlag, 1988.
3. Francois Bancilhon et al., "The Design and Implementation of O_2, an Object-Oriented Database System," *Lecture Notes in Computer Science, Advances in Object-Oriented Database Systems, 2nd International Workshop on Object-Oriented Database Systems,* Springer-Verlag, 1988.

9

ObjectStore

Introduction

This chapter is dedicated to exploring the popular commercial OODBMS ObjectStore. ObjectStore is widely used in industry for engineering databases, CAD/CAM, etc. In this chapter, the Object-Store architecture and its features, programming interfaces, and querying capabilities are described in great detail. Programming examples using the C++ programming interface are presented.

9.1 The ObjectStore OODBMS

ObjectStore is an object-oriented database system developed by Object Design, Inc. It provides persistent storage for objects. It provides support for object identity and can store arbitrary types of data. Data can be accessed by navigational or associative access. Object-Store facilitates the creation and maintenance of multiple versions of data, and provides support for version history.

Persistence and versioning in ObjectStore are orthogonal to type. ObjectStore facilitates development of a distributed versioned persistent memory. It provides a DML as well as a C and C++ interface to the persistent data. It supports optimized precompiled and run-time queries.

The compile-time type checking of C++ applies to persistent as well as transient objects. ObjectStore is designed so that the speed of dereferencing of pointers to persistent objects is almost as fast as the speed of dereferencing a pointer to a transient object, which is the speed of a single load instruction.

9.2 ObjectStore Data Organization

ObjectStore stores persistent data on disks, in ObjectStore file systems. The file system can be either raw partitions or the standard

UNIX file system. Databases are made up of segments. Segments are variable-sized regions of memory that can be used as the unit of transfer from persistent storage to the memory space of the application. Segments are in turn made up of pages.

Databases are organized into logical directories, similar to the organization of UNIX directories. However, ObjectStore directories are independent of the UNIX directory hierarchies, and are only logical structures.

A single application can access multiple databases. In fact, the databases accessed can even be on different file systems, handled by different ObjectStore Servers (Servers are explained below).

9.3 ObjectStore Processes

ObjectStore requires three auxiliary processes in order to provide an execution environment to applications (Fig. 9.1). They are the *Object-Store Server,* the *Directory Manager,* and the *Cache Manager.* The Server handles all access to ObjectStore file systems. It handles storage and retrieval of persistent data. The Directory Manager can be used to manage ObjectStore directory hierarchies. It is used to maintain permission modes, creation dates, owners, and groups. A Cache Manager is used to manage an application's client cache. When an application starts, the Cache Manager is started automatically. All three of these ObjectStore processes are usually started when the machine boots, and most users never have to worry about starting or stopping them.

9.4 ObjectStore Distributed Database Architecture

ObjectStore supports a client/server model of computing, with user applications being clients and the ObjectStore Servers providing the functionality of distributed databases (Fig. 9.2). It is possible to have

---

1. ObjectStore Server: Manages data pages on behalf of client applications

2. ObjectStore Directory Manager: Maps hierarchical database names to servers

3. ObjectStore Cache Manager: Responsible for optimization of page-lock management on behalf of client applications

---

Figure 9.1   ObjectStore process architecture.

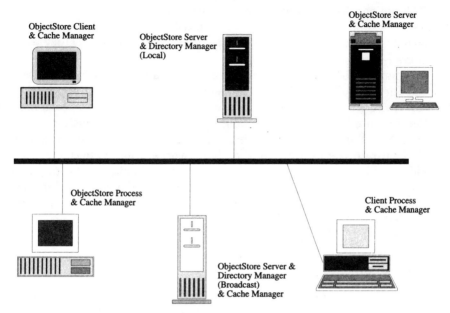

Figure 9.2 ObjectStore distributed database architecture.

one Server per machine, and there can be several servers in a network. Each Server manages several databases on behalf of client applications. The databases can be stored in raw disk partitions or on file systems. The servers are multithreaded, with one thread of execution dedicated to an active client. When client applications select pages to read or write, the ObjectStore Server makes the pages available.

Since a Server can handle several databases and there can be several Servers on the network, it is important to be able to locate the required database. Such a service is provided by the Directory Manager, which is responsible for mapping hierarchical database names to Servers. The association is typically logical, not physical. The directory structure of databases is similar to the UNIX directory structure. However, databases in the same directory can be physically located on different Servers on the same network. The Directory Manager is responsible for mapping a database name to an ObjectStore Server when a client opens a database. Directory Managers are associated with a Server, and they store the database names on that Server.

Directory Managers are of two types:

1. Local Mode
2. Broadcast Mode

There can be only one Broadcast Mode Directory Manager in each network, and it handles requests to locate databases on Servers. It is possible to address requests to specific Local Mode Directory Managers.

When a client application tries to access data pages from Servers, the Servers supply locks and pages as needed. The client applications can cache the pages and locks between transactions. It is possible for Servers to reclaim locks from client applications once the clients have no use for them. Such reclaiming can be done using a "lazy" approach. To facilitate the caching at the client workstation, ObjectStore provides for a Cache Manager. Typically, there is one Cache Manager per machine. The Cache Manager and the client applications can communicate using shared memory. Client applications and a Server can be on the same machine.

9.5 ObjectStore Memory Mapping Architecture

ObjectStore has employed a virtual memory model, where persistent data are transferred between database memory and program memory automatically and transparently to the user. When an application's running program refers to data that are persistent in the database, ObjectStore detects such references and automatically transfers the segment that contains the referenced data to the application's cache. The page that contains the referenced data is then brought into the virtual memory. The whole process is similar to demand paging. Instead of a page fault, an *object fault* triggers mapping data into virtual memory.

Any access to the persistent object whose pointer is so far unmapped triggers a violation in the operating system, which is then handled by a violation handler in ObjectStore that performs the data transfer and virtual memory mapping.

9.6 ObjectStore Data Manipulation Language (DML)

The DML has the support for the following features:

- Persistent storage class specifier
- Indexable member declarations
- Inverse member declaration
- Query expression
- Path expression
- For each statement

■ Transaction statement

9.7 Persistence in ObjectStore

Persistence in ObjectStore is orthogonal to type. The same kind of data can be both persistent and transient. Persistent data can be accessed directly and transparently within C++ programs. One way to specify persistent data involves an overloading of the C++ new operator to allow creation of heap_based persistent objects. It also allows for the specification of clustering information using the database segment. Another way of specifying persistent data is also used to create objects that serve as database entry points. The storage class specifier persistent provides this second way of specifying persistence:

```
persistent <control-variable> class_type object-name;
```

where control-variable specifies the database in which the variable's storage is to reside.

9.8 Database Creation

The database names are like names of UNIX files, and all names begin with "/". To create an ObjectStore database using its C++ interface, the create member function of database type objects is invoked, with proper permissions specified, as indicated below:

```
database *db = database::create("/usr1/dir1/db1", 0664, 1);
```

The access permissions of 0664 are similar to octals used to specify UNIX file access permissions. The create function takes a pathname as shown above.

9.9 Opening and Closing the Objectstore Database

Databases can be opened using the open() member function as shown below:

```
database *db = database::open("/usr1/dir1/db1", 0, 0664);
```

The first argument is a UNIX-like pathname. It can be preceded by the name of a host machine followed by a pair of colons "::". The second argument is used to specify the read or write mode of opening the database. If the database does not yet exist, the open() member function will create one, if possible.

Databases need not be explicitly closed in applications. ObjectStore will close all open databases when a program exits. Explicit database closes can be performed as shown below:

```
db->close();
```

9.10 Database Roots

Database roots are necessary to locate application objects starting with a named application object. Each database allows for a set of roots with a flat name space. After accessing the named root object, applications can navigate to other objects associated with that root. Root objects can be created and accessed using the DML or the library interface. The keyword persistent is used in the DML to specify objects that behave as root objects. The persistent keyword is used as a syntactic interface which provides transparent lookup/initialization of root objects while mapping them to program variables.

Applications can call functions to look up root objects, and subsequently get/set values, using the C++/C library interface. The class database_root is part of the C++ interface, and its member function create_root can be used to create a root with the specified name:

```
database_root *r = db->create_root("docs");
```

9.11 Clustering

For better performance in terms of object access time, objects that are generally processed together or those that are dependent on each other can be clustered together. When related objects are clustered, they can be simultaneously retrieved from secondary storage and cached together, thus resulting in fewer server, disk, and network interactions. Since the clustered objects are placed close to each other, they can be read/write-locked together, which also results in fewer server and network interactions. Clustering can be employed to optimize a specific set of access patterns.

In ObjectStore, clustering can be carried out at three different levels:

1. Clustering in the same database
2. Clustering in the same segment
3. Clustering on the same page

9.12 Transactions

Transactions are the means of implementing atomicity of database access and updates. Database contents can be accessed only within a transaction. ObjectStore transactions can be lexically scoped or dynamically scoped. Lexical scoping can be performed by means of the DML function

```
do_transaction() {…}
```

or by means of the library interface macros

```
OS_BEGIN_TXN() … OS_END_TXN()
```

Transactions can be of type `read_only` or `update`. Read-only transactions will not be able to modify persistent data. The following is an example of an update transaction:

```
OS_BEGIN_TXN(t1,0, transaction::update)
…
OS_END_TXN(t1)
```

The first argument for the macro `OS_BEGIN_TXN` is a unique label, the second is a pointer to an exception variable, and the third is an enum specifying either `transaction::update` or `transaction::read_only`.

When transactions deadlock, the ObjectStore server will choose a deadlock victim using one of the following four deadlock resolution techniques: *current, age, work, random.* The deadlock victim's transaction will be retried, if possible. Otherwise it will be aborted. Only lexically scoped transactions can be retried.

When transactions are dynamically scoped, objects of class `transaction` are manipulated by applications by means of member functions called to begin, commit, or abort transactions. Dynamic transactions are useful when the application code does not permit a lexical scoping, as in user-interface callback code. The `transaction` class provides for `begin()` and `commit()` static member functions that are used to start and commit transactions dynamically. `transaction::begin()` returns a pointer to a transaction type object, an instance of class `transaction.transaction::commit()` takes a pointer to a transaction as an argument.

Pointers to persistent data can be set when persistent data are accessed within a transaction. Such pointers cannot be assigned in one transaction and then used in another. References should be used instead of pointers when persistent data are accessed across transactions. References are valid across transactions. Parameterized references can be treated like pointers.

If the transaction does not commit but aborts, changes to the persistent data are undone or rolled back.

9.13   Nested Transactions

ObjectStore permits nested transactions. If we want to roll back changes in persistent data to their state as of some point after the beginning of a transaction, we can use a nested transaction that starts at this later pointer within the first transaction.

When the outermost transaction commits, all the inner transactions also commit. The transaction types of all inner transactions must match the outermost transaction type. Until the topmost transaction commits, the database updates made in nested transactions are not visible outside the process. When a nested transaction is aborted, persistent data are rolled back to their state as of the beginning of that transaction. However, no locks are released until the topmost-level transaction terminates.

9.14   Locks

Locks in ObjectStore are transparently acquired when they are needed. When persistent data are initially accessed for read/write within a transaction, this is detected, and the ObjectStore server is consulted to acquire the necessary locks. Read locks are updated to write locks automatically after the first attempt to update the data. When a process writes a data item, the page or segment on which the data item resides is *write-locked*. This prevents other processes from reading or writing to that page or segment.

The smallest granularity of locking is a page. Data can be locked at segment or page level. Locking and unlocking of objects is transparent to the programmer and is completely automatic.

9.15   Schema

ObjectStore stores information in each database about the classes of objects stored there, along with the layout of instances of these classes. Such schema information is stored as C++ objects. ObjectStore generates representations of classes at compile time, in order to manage database memory. The schema generated at compile time is stored as persistent data by using ObjectStore's database management capabilities.

9.16   Schema Evolution

Over time, in most applications, the definition of classes changes. Changing the definition of a class or a data type could result in a change in the size and layout of its instances. In some situations, there could be a significant number of instances of the changed classes. Updating all the persistent objects to make them conform to newer class definitions may not be easy or cost-effective. However, the OODBMS should provide mechanisms for migrating old objects from old databases to conform to the newer definitions, or provide some facilities by which applications compiled with the newer class definitions could access existing databases.

Schema evolution can be defined to be the process of updating a database to make it compatible with a new application schema (Fig. 9.3). Typically, the programmer redefines the classes by editing appropriate header files and source code. The changed code is recompiled, and a newer version of the application is created. There is generally no restriction on the types of changes. Thus, the application schema is easily updated.

After a new application schema is created, the programmer can invoke schema evolution to migrate instances in existing databases. Most simple changes can be handled automatically by ObjectStore. ObjectStore provides a utility called `ossevol` to handle generic changes. For application-specific changes that cannot be handled automatically by ObjectStore, the programmer has to write conversion programs using the class libraries provided for that purpose.

The migration of existing data to make them conform to new class definitions can be done in a batch mode. In fact, entire databases can be migrated.

9.17   ODI/ObjectStore Database Example Application: Document Store

In this section, an application that uses ObjectStore to save persistent data is described, and the code to implement it is presented. The explanation of ObjectStore database issues follows the example.

The application is designed to create a persistent collection of document objects such that paragraphs in the documents (referred to as segments here) can be accessed at random, if necessary.

1. Schema can be modified by programmer to reflect changes in class definitions.

2. New instances of modified classes can be easily handled. Programmer provides proper initialization for instances.

3. Instances of modified classes in existing databases must be migrated. One way to migrate is the "lazy" approach.

4. Programmer can optionally provide transformer functions to migrate objects.

Figure 9.3   Schema evolution.

The segments and the documents are specified by the classes segment and document, respectively.

```
class segment{
  public:
    char *text;
};

class document{
  public:
    segment segs[NUM_SEGS];
};
```

The schema must be declared using the macro OS_MARK_SCHEMA_
TYPE, as shown below:

```
/*
 * schema.cc:
 */
#include <ostore/ostore.hh>
#include <ostore/coll.hh>
#include <ostore/manschem.hh>
#include "simple.hh"
static void dummy () {
  OS_MARK_SCHEMA_TYPE(document);
  OS_MARK_SCHEMA_TYPE(segment);
}
```

The document objects could be stored in an array. The creation and
population of the database of documents is shown in the code below. A
segment is just a character string encapsulated as an object, and NUM_
SEGS segments are stored in each document object. To speed up the
process of database population, it might help to limit the number of
object creations in each transaction. Thus, the number of transactions
and the number of documents created per transaction are command-
line parameters, stored in the variables ntix and docs_per_tix,
respectively. For simplicity, the same document (passed as a command-
line argument) is opened for reading during document creation. Thus,
all the documents will be the same one. In the program listed below,
the function TRACE_SCOPE() is used for creating timestamps to measure the time taken by different activities. It is not part of ObjectStore.

```
/*
 * creat.C: Creates the databases for different document
 *                    sources
 *
 */

#include <ostore/ostore.hh> // ObjectStore system header file
#include <string.h>
#include <iostream.h>
#include <stdlib.h>
#include "trace.h"
```

```
#define DOCS_PER_TXN (10)
#define STR_SIZE 1024

#include "simple.hh"

getstr(char *buffer, FILE *fd)
{
  const MAX_LINE_LEN = 300;
  char str[MAX_LINE_LEN + 1];

  buffer[0] = '\0';
  for (int i = 0; i < 10; i++) {
    if (fgets(str, MAX_LINE_LEN, fd))
      strcat(buffer, str);
  }
}

main( int argc, char** argv)
{
  if (argc < 9) {
    fprintf(stderr, "Usage: %s start_num end_num host path
      input_filename docs_per_tix ntix outfile \n",
      argv[0]);
    exit(1);
  }

      /* Store Command Line parameters */
    int start_num = atoi(argv[1]);
    int end_num = atoi(argv[2]);
    char* host = argv[3];
    char* path = argv[4];
    char* filename = argv[5];
    int docs_per_tix = atoi(argv[6]);
    int ntix = atoi(argv[7]);
    char* ofile = argv[8];

    TRACE_SCOPE("Creating database");

    for(int i = start_num; i < end_num + 1; i++) {
        /* creating Document Source names */
      const char *source = "DOC_SRC_";
      char doc_source[60], intstr[20];

      strcpy(doc_source, path);
      strcat(doc_source, "/");
      strcat(doc_source, source);
      sprintf(intstr, "%d", i);
      strcat(doc_source, intstr);
      cout << "Creating database: " << doc_source <0< endl << flush;
      database *db = database::create(doc_source, 0664, 1);
      reference<document*> docs;

      OS_BEGIN_TXN(t1,0, transaction::update)
      database_root *r = db->create_root("docs");
      os_typespec doc_star("document*");
      docs = new(db, docs_per_tix * ntix, &doc_star)
              document*[docs_per_tix * ntix];
      r->set_value(docs, &doc_star);
      OS_END_TXN(t1)

    int doc = 0;
    for (int tix = 0; tix < ntix; tix++) // ntix transactions of type
```

```
        t2 below
      {
      OS_BEGIN_TXN(t2,0,transaction::update)
      for(int d = 0; d < docs_per_tix; d++) // creating docs_per_tix
documents
        {
        document *adoc = new(db->create_segment(),
          document::get_os_typespec()) document;
        ((document**) docs)[doc++] = adoc;

        FILE *fd;
        if ((fd = fopen(filename, "r")) = = NULL)
        {
          fprintf(stderr, "Can't open %s in docobj()\n",
            filename);
          return 0;
        }

        for(int j = 0; j < NUM_SEGS; j++)
        {
          char savestr[2000];
          getstr(savestr, fd);
          adoc->segs[j].text = new(segment::of(adoc),
            strlen(savestr), os_typespec::get_char())
          char[strlen(savestr)];
          //cout << "String is:" << savestr << endl;
          strcpy(adoc->segs[j].text, savestr);
        }
        fclose(fd);
      }
      OS_END_TXN(t2);
    }
    db->close();
    myTrace.out();
  }
  myTrace.out();
}
```

The function get str() is used to access lines of text that are stored in the segments of the document. In the transaction t1, the array of documents docs is created and is named as a root object "docs" in the database. The member function set_value() is used to assign an object as a root object after create_root() creates a root object.

The database::create_root() function requires you to specify the name to be associated with an entry point, but the entry point itself is specified in a separate call, using the function database_root::set_value().

```
OS_BEGIN_TXN(t1,0, transaction::update)
database_root *r = db->create_root("docs");
os_typespec doc_star("document*");
docs = new(db, docs_per_tix * ntix, &doc_star)
      document*[docs_per_tix * ntix];
r->set_value(docs, &doc_star);
OS_END_TXN(t1)
```

The pair of macros OS_BEGIN_TXN and OS_END_TXN helps specify the scope of the transactions. The class os_typespec is used to specify the type of the object that is to be created and in other functions such as set_value, where it is used to specify the type of the root object. Instances of os_typespec are passed to persistent new by applications using the ObjectStore C++ library interface. Once an os_typespec for a particular type is created, it can be used to create all the program's new instances of that type, and there is no need to create a separate os_typespec for each call to new.

A persistent array is created in the database as shown below:

```
docs = new(db, docs_per_tix * ntix, &doc_star)
       document*[docs_per_tix * ntix];
```

This call to new allocates and initializes an array of docs_per_tix * ntix document objects. The third argument to new is an os_typespec for the documents.

9.18   Accessing Persistent Data from the Database

After the database of documents has been populated, the data can be accessed by first opening the database and locating the required entry point. The database can be opened as follows:

```
database *db = database::open(path);
```

where path is the string specifying the UNIX-like path of the database. The array of documents created in the previous example had been stored with the root named as "docs". The code below shows how the root object can be retrieved:

```
document **docarr = (document **)
db->find_root("docs")->get_value();
```

This code shows that persistent objects can be looked up using the database::find_root() function. This function takes an argument that is a root's name. If the root with that name exists, a pointer to it is returned. The function database_root::getvalue() is called to retrieve a pointer to the actual entry point object pointed to be the root object. The pointer to the entry point associated with the root is obtained by typecasting the void* returned by get_value(). Thus, the void* returned by database_root::getvalue() is later typecast into the type of the entry point object, in this case, a document**.

The array of documents retrieved above can be indexed to get to the required document and to the required segment within the document as shown below:

```
char *str = docarr[doc_num]->segs[seg].text;
cout << ":Text :" << str << endl;
```

where `doc_num` and `seg` are the document index and the segment index, respectively.

Since the access of the persistent data (document) should be performed within a transaction, the code should be as shown below:

```
database *db = database::open(cdi_source);

OS_BEGIN_TXN(t1,0, transaction::read_only)
  document **docarr = (document **)
  db->find_root("docs")->get_value();
  char *str = docarr[doc_num]->segs[seg].text;
  cout << ":Text :" << str << endl;
OS_END_TXN(t1)
```

where `seg` and `doc_num` are integer variables specifying the required indices for segment retrieval. Note that the transaction `t1` above is a `read_only` transaction.

9.19   Creating Segments in ObjectStore Databases

Every database, by default, has only one segment initially, called the *default segment*. When new objects are created, there are two ways to specify where they are to be stored: by specifying the database or by specifying a segment for the new object.

When a segment is specified, it helps enforce *clustering* of objects. Segments, in ObjectStore, are of variable sizes and can be as large as required. A segment is the unit of transfer of data from database storage to memory. Clustering using segments provides *locality of reference*.

If there is a need to create a new segment in the database, it can be created explicitly using the member function `database::create_segment()`. In the previous programming example of creating the document store, the `database::create_segment()` member function was invoked as follows:

```
document *adoc = new(db->create_segment(),
document::get_os_typespec()) document;
```

The `db->create_segment()` member function returns a pointer to an instance of the system-supplied class `segment`.

9.20   Collections, Sets, and Bags

A collection, in ObjectStore, is an object that facilitates grouping together other objects. Collections can be used for several purposes: for modeling many-valued attributes, for creating "class extents," etc. Collection classes come with member functions for inserting objects into collections, removing objects from the collections, and retrieving objects from the collections, as well as functions that help determine the cardinality of collections.

The ObjectStore collection facility provides a great deal of control over the behavior and representation of the collections used in typical applications. Collections can be ordered or unordered. There are several implementations of collections to choose from. The collection's representation may change in response to changes in the cardinality of the collection. Thus, the actual implementation can be automatically selected by the system or explicitly specified by the user. In Object-Store, the instances of os_collection class can be implemented using one of the following:

1. os_packed_list, when ordered

2. os_ptr_hash, when unordered

3. os_ordered_hash, when ordered and maintain cursors

4. os_tinyarray

Collections can be implemented using parameterized types. The classes derived from parameterized collection classes can also be parameterized classes. ObjectStore collection classes come in both parameterized and nonparameterized flavors. The creation of parameterized collection class objects is shown below:

```
os_Collection <element*> &myelements;
myelements = os_Collection<element*>::create(db1);
```

The os_Collection::create() member function returns a reference to a collection, which is assigned to a variable of type os_Collection<element*>&. In the example above, element is a class of objects and db1 is a pointer to an object of class database.

Collections are an alternative to aggregation data structures like linked lists, arrays, etc. Collections come in several forms—sets, bags, and lists (Fig. 9.4).

The simplest type of ObjectStore collection is the *set*. The members of a set are unordered. Thus, sets are used when the order of objects grouped in a set is unimportant. As stated before, sets can be both parameterized and nonparameterized. Parameterized sets belong to the ObjectStore class os_Set, while nonparameterized sets are

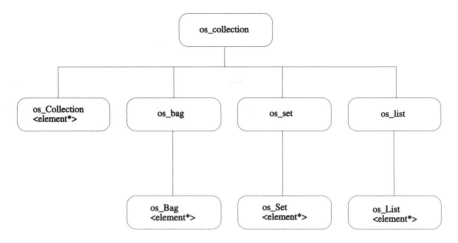

Figure 9.4 Collection class hierarchy.

instances of class os_set. In general, parameterized classes have a parameter for constraining the type of values allowable as elements. The *element type parameter* is specified in angle brackets as shown below:

```
os_Set <element*> *myelms;
```

Notice that the element type is a pointer type. In this example, myelms is a pointer to a set of "pointers to element." The set can be created, as shown below, using the static create() member function with a database* db (pointer to a database) as an clustering argument.

```
myelms = &os_Set<element*>::create(db);
```

Element objects can be inserted into the set myelms as shown below:

```
el1 = new(seg, element_type) element(buffer, seg, strvar)
myelms->insert(el1);
```

Sets and collections are provided with member functions to traverse them with iterations. Iterations can be performed by means of a *cursor,* an instance of the parameterized class os_Cursor, associated with the collection to be traversed. The class os_Cursor has member functions first(), next(), and more() to facilitate traversal.

9.21 Indexable Members of a Set

When a set or collection of like items is created, it can be indexed by certain data members of the items. Data members of a given class are established as indexable by adding to the class the declaration of a data member of that class whose value is os_backptr. This declaration must precede the declaration of the data members intended to be indexable. For each indexable member, a call is made to the macro os_indexable_member with the name of the class containing the member and the name and type of the member that should be indexable as arguments:

```
os_backptr b;
os_indexable_member(element,eid,char *) eid;
```

The os_backptr member of a class is used to establish other members of the class as indexable. In the module where the member functions of the class are defined, for each indexable member of the class, a call to the macro os_indexable_body is made, with the name of the class, the name and the type of the indexable member, and the os_index macro specifying the os_backptr member as arguments:

```
os_indexable_body(element,eid,char *,os_index(element,b));
```

9.22   Document Store Example Revisited: Using Sets

In this section, the document store example will be further developed to incorporate the facilities of ObjectStore sets. The application classes are also redefined to provide a better design of document objects. Information source elements (ISE) are objects which have references to document objects. Documents consist of many elements which are stored in a set. The set of elements that make up a document is created by the constructor of the document. Elements are the new objects that replace the segments of the previous example and contain a persistent string called text.

The element class has a persistent string data member called text. It is a data member of type _Pers_string, which is defined in pstring.hh. Class element has one indexable member called eid. Note the os_backptr data member b, which precedes the declaration of eid. Class element has one constructor, which takes in a string as the first argument, in addition to a segment specifying clustering and a string for the eid member.

The classes docobj, element, and ise are defined in the file simple.hh, which is listed below:

```
/* simple.hh : Class Definitions */

#include <ostore/pstring.hh>
#include <ostore/coll.hh>
```

```
class docobj;
class element;

class element {
  public:
    _Pers_string text;
    os_backptr b;
    os_indexable_member(element,eid,char *) eid;
    static os_typespec* get_os_typespec();
    element(char *str, segment *seg, char *eidster);
    setelement(char *str){text = str;};
    getelement(char *str){
       strcpy(str, (const char *)text); };
};

class docobj {
  public:
    static os_typespec* get_os_typespec();
    os_Set <element*> *myelms;
    docobj(database *db, segment *seg, int, int, char *, char *);
    getElement(_Pers_string &);
    putElement(_Pers_string &);
};

class ise {
  public:
    static os_typespec* get_os_typespec();
    os_backptr b;
    os_indexable_member(ise,name,char *) name;
    docobj *body;
    _Pers_string type;
    _Pers_string status;
    _Pers_string memo;
    ise(database *, segment *, int, int, char *filename, char *oid-
var);

};
```

Class docobj has a set of elements myelms that make up a document. It also has a constructor, which is responsible for creating and populating the set of elements myelms.

The class ise has an indexable member, name, which is used to identify and locate the ise object. It also has a pointer to the actual document object, the data member body of type docobj. The constructor of ise is responsible for the creation and population of the document object whose pointer is assigned to body.

The constructor of ise is as listed below:

```
#include <ostore/ostore.hh> // ObjectStore system header file
#include <string.h>
#include <iostream.h>

#include "simple.hh"
/*
*   ise.cc : Definition of ise class member functions
*/

#include <ostore/ostore.hh> // ObjectStore system header file
#include <ostore/pstring.hh>
```

```
os_indexable_body(ise,name,char *,os_index(ise,b));

     // Creating the object from file
ise::ise(database *db, segment *seg, int num_segs, int num_lines,
      char *filename, char *oidvar)
{
  body = new(seg, docobj::get_os_typespec())
                  docobj(db, seg, num_segs, num_lines,
                      filename, oidvar);
  name = new(seg, 20, os_typespec::get_char()) char[20];
  strcpy((char *)name, oidvar);
}
```

The constructor of ise creates a new docobj and stores a pointer
to it in body. The name of the document is also copied into the indexable data member name.

The constructor of docobj is as listed below:

```
/*
 * docobj.C: Definition of the docobj class member functions
 */

#include <ostore/ostore.hh>
#include <ostore/coll.hh>
#include <ostore/pstring.hh>
#include <stdlib.h>
#include <iostream.h>
#include <stdio.h>
#include "simple.hh" //User DDL schema header file

#define NUM_SEGS 200
#define NUM_LINES 1

int char_rank( const void * arg1, const void *arg2);

docobj::docobj(database *db, segment *seg, int num_segs,
            int num_lines, char *filename, char *oidvar)
{
  const MAX_LINE_LEN = 300;
  char buffer[2000];
  char str[MAX_LINE_LEN + 1];

  os_typespec *element_type = new os_typespec("element");
  // Now parse the text in the file, and insert
  // segments into set.

  char strvar[60], intstr[20];

  FILE *fd;
  if ((fd = fopen(filename, "r")) = = NULL) {
    fprintf(stderr, "Can't open %s in docobj()\n", filename);
    return;
}

  myelms = &os_Set<element*>::create(db);
  os_index_path &key_spec = os_index_path::create("element*",
            "eid", db);

  os_index_key(char *, char_rank, 0);

  myelms->add_index(key_spec);
```

```
for(int segments = 0; segments < num_segs; segments++)
{
  strcpy(buffer, "");

  for (int i = 0; i<num_lines; i++)
    {
    if (fgets(str, MAX_LINE_LEN, fd))
      strcat(buffer, str);
    }

  strcpy(strvar, "segid");
  sprintf(intstr, "%d", segments);
  strcat(strvar, intstr);

  myelms->insert(new(seg, element_type) element(buffer, seg, str-
var));
  }
  fclose(fd);
}
```

The docobj::docobj() constructor is responsible for parsing the
input file and then creating the set of elements. The input file is first
opened to read the elements of the document. A set is created, and a
pointer to it is assigned to myelms. An os_index_path object is created to specify index keys to enable query optimization. Each path
specifies a certain kind of mapping by specifying a sequence of data
member names. The os_index_key macro is used to register user-
defined rank and hash functions with ObjectStore. The set myelms is
provided with an index by means of the add_index() function as
shown below:

```
myelms->add_index(key_spec);
```

For simplicity, a sequence of num_lines lines is read from the
input file and concatenated to create each element. The buffer
which holds the concatenated string is used to create a new element
object. The element object is then inserted into the set.

```
myelms->insert(new(seg, element_type) element(buffer, seg,
    strvar));
```

The constructor of the element class is as shown below:

```
#include <ostore/ostore.hh> // ObjectStore system header file
#include <string.h>
#include <iostream.h>

#include "simple.hh"
  /*
   * element.cc : Definition of ise class member functions
   */

#include <ostore/ostore.hh> // ObjectStore system·header file
#include <ostore/pstring.hh>
```

```
os_indexable_body(element,eid,char *,os_index(element,b));

element::element(char *str, segment *seg, char *oldster)
{
  text = str;
  eid = new(seg, 20, os_typespec::get_char()) char[20];
  strcpy(eid, oldster);
};
```

The constructor of `element` copies the argument `str` into the persistent string object `text`. It also creates a new `char` array and copies the argument `oldster` into the indexable data member `eid`.

The creation of the document store databases and the population of these databases can be done as shown below:

```
/*
 * creat.cc: Creates the databases for Document Sources
 * Populates the document databases
 * Bindu Rama Rao
 *
 */

#include <ostore/ostore.hh> // ObjectStore system header file
#include <ostore/coll.hh>
#include <string.h>
#include <iostream.h>
#include <stdlib.h>
#include "trace.h"

#define DOCS_PER_TXN (10)
#define STR_SIZE 1024

#include "simple.hh"
#include <ostore/pstring.hh>

int char_rank( const void * arg1, const void *arg2)
{
  const char *p1 = (const char * ) arg1;
  const char *p2 = (const char * ) arg2;
  return(strcmp(p1,p2));
}

main( int argc, char** argv)
{
  if (argc < 11) {
    fprintf(stderr, "Usage: %s start_num end_num host path
input_filename docs_per_tix ntix outfile num_segs num_lines \n",
        argv[0]);
    exit(1);
  }

  int start_num = atoi(argv[1]);
  int end_num = atoi(argv[2]);
  char* host = argv[3];
  char* path = argv[4];
  char* filename = argv[5];
  int docs_per_tix = atoi(argv[6]);
  int ntix = atoi(argv[7]);
  char* ofile = argv[8];
```

```
int num_segs = atoi(argv[9]);
int num_lines = atoi(argv[10]);

os_Set<ise*> *ises = 0; // set that stores ise instances
os_typespec *ise_type = new os_typespec("ise");

for(int i = start_num; i < end_num + 1; i++)
{
    /* creating Document Source names */
    const char *source = "DOC_SRC_";
char doc_source[60], intstr[20];

strcpy(doc_source, path);
strcat(doc_source, "/");
strcat(doc_source, source);
sprintf(intstr, "%d", i);
strcat(doc_source, intstr);
cout << "Creating database: " << doc_source << endl << flush;

database *db = database::create(doc_source, 0664, 1);
cout << "database created, need to populate: " << doc_source <<
endl << flush;

OS_BEGIN_TXN(t1,0, transaction::update)

    ises = &os_Set<ise*>::create(db);
    database_root *r = db->create_root("docs");
    r->set_value(ises);
    os_index_path &key_spec = os_index_path::create("ise*",
      "name", db);
    os_index_key(char *, char_rank, 0);
    ises->add_index(key_spec);
    int doc = 0;
    char oidvar[30];
    segment *seg = db->create_segment();
    for (int tix = 0; tix < ntix; tix++)
    {
      for(int d = 0; d < docs_per_tix; d++)
        {
        strcpy(oidvar, "oid");
        sprintf(intstr, "%d", doc++);
        strcat(oidvar, intstr);
                // Create instances of ise
        ise *aise = new(seg, ise_type)
                    ise((database *)db, seg, num_segs,
                    num_lines, filename, oidvar);
        if (ises != NULL)
          ises->insert(aise);
      }
      }
      db->close();
    OS_END_TXN(t1)
  }
}
```

In the example above, a set ise is created to hold ise objects,
and instances of class ise are created in a loop. The constructor of
ise creates an instance of docobj. The constructor of docobj in

turn creates a set and populates it with element objects. The newly created ise object is inserted into a set pointed to by ises, as shown below:

```
ise *aise = new(seg, ise_type)
ise((database *)db, seg, num_segs,
   num_lines, filename, oidvar);
if (ises ! = NULL)
   ises->insert(aise);
```

9.23   Database Lookups Using Query Objects

ObjectStore databases can be queried using either the DML interface or the C++ library interface. The DML query interface provides query syntax for compile-time parsing of query expressions. The C++ library interface provides for run-time parsing and run-time evaluation of queries. Queries are usually addressed to specific collections of data to retrieve all items in the collection for which the query expression is true. In both the DML and the C++ library interface, it is possible to retrieve either a transient collection containing all elements for which the expression is true or a single element for which the expression is true.

The query expression should be valid C++ syntax. A DML query to retrieve from a collection of addresses an address with zip code of 60185 and a telephone area code of 708 can be as follows:

```
os_Set <address*> addrset;
address* adr1 = addrset[:zip = = 60185 && area_code = = 708:];
```

[::] is ObjectStore syntax for DML queries. The expression contained in it serves as a selection predicate, and is conceptually applied to each object in the set. Query expressions can be nested. The [::] syntax is a language extension.

The C++ library interface provides for query strings applied to collections directly so that they are parsed as C++ query expressions, optimized, and executed at run time. The translation of the query expression is separated from its execution.

The following sequence of events is part of the query processing (see Fig. 9.5):

1. Translation of the query string

2. Binding of free reference values

3. Execution against a particular collection

---

1. It is possible to separate the query translation and execution. The steps are:

   a. Translation of the query string
   b. Binding of free reference values
   c. Execution of the query against a particular collection

2. `os_coll_query` object can be used to translate a query string.

3. The `os_coll_query` object should then be bound to an `os_bound_query` object so that free references, if any, can be given values. The values are specified using a list of `os_keyword_arg` objects.

4. The instances of `os_bound_query` can then be applied to one or more collections.

Figure 9.5   Query objects and query manipulations.

The query expressions (strings) may contain references to objects and functions not known to the translation schema. If there are *free references* in the query string, the type of these free references must be specified by `type_cast`.

Instances of class `os_coll_query` are used to translate a query string. The specification of the `os_coll_query` object requires a string denoting the element type of the collection or set, a string specifying the query, and the database against which the query is to be validated.

```
const os_coll_query& q2 =
   os_coll_query::create_pick("element*",
     "strcmp(eid, (char *)elemstr)",
                  database::transient_database);
```

In the code above, the specification of `database::transient_database` indicates that the application schema `db` should be used for validation. The `os_coll_query` object is then bound to an `os_bound_query` object. Instances of class `os_bound_query` are query objects built from instances of class `os_coll_query` and `os_keyword_arg`.

```
os_bound_query bq2(q2, (os_keyword_arg("elemstr", elemstr)));
```

Free references, if any, in the query string are given values with a list of `os_keyword_args`. Instances of class `os_keyword_arg` are used in specifying query bindings.

```
os_keyword_arg("elemstr", elemstr);
```

The os_bound_query instance is then applied to one or more collections as shown below:

```
myelms->query_pick(bq2);
```

Collections and sets are provided with the member functions query() and query_pick() to retrieve either a collection (set) or a single item, as a result of evaluating a query.

The following program, access.cc, provides a good example of the use of query objects to retrieve objects from the ObjectStore database.

```
/*
 * access.cc: In a loop, access an element from
 *                 all ises (documents) from a document source
 *                 (database).
 */

#include <ostore/ostore.hh> // ObjectStore system header file
#include <ostore/coll.hh> // ObjectStore system header file
#include <string.h>
#include <iostream.h>
#include <stdlib.h>
#include "trace.h"

#define DOCS_PER_TXN (10)
#define STR_SIZE 1024

#include "simple.hh"

main( int argc, char** argv)
{
  if (argc < 4) {
    fprintf(stderr, "Usage: %s document_num seg num_docs path \n",
    argv[0]);
    exit(1);
  }

  int document_num = atoi(argv[1]);
  int seg = atoi(argv[2]);
  int num_docs = atoi(argv[3]);
  char *path = argv[4];

  const char *source = "DOC_SRC_";
  char doc_source[60], intstr[20], elemstr[20];
  strcpy(doc_source, path);
  strcat(doc_source, "/");
  strcat(doc_source, source);
  sprintf(intstr, "%d", document_num);
  strcat(doc_source, intstr);

  const os_coll_query& q2 =
    os_coll_query::create_pick("element*",
      "strcmp(eid, (char *)elemstr)",
                        database::transient_database);
```

```
cout << "Starting access of Document Source:"
    << doc_source << ":" << time(0) << "\n";

OS_BEGIN_TXN(t1,0, transaction::read_only)
    database *db = database::open(doc_source);
    ise *p;
    char str[2000];
    strcpy(elemstr, "segid");
    sprintf(intstr, "%d", seg);
    strcat(elemstr, intstr);
    os_bound_query bq2(q2, (os_keyword_arg("elemstr", elemstr)));

    os_Set<ise*> &ises = (*(os_Set<ise*>*)
        (db->find_root("docs")->get_value()));
        cout << "Set ises accessed" << endl;
    os_Cursor <ise*> c(ises);

    int doc = 0;
    foreach (p, ises)
    {
        element *ep;
        if ((ep = p->body->myelms->query_pick(bq2)) != 0)
        {
            ep->getelement(str);
            cout << doc++ << str << endl;
        }
    }

    db->close();
OS_END_TXN(t1)

}
```

In the example shown above, the query string uses the `strcmp`
function as part of the expression:

```
"strcmp(eid, (char *)elemstr)"
```

The root of the database is first accessed using the
`database::find_root()` member function, which retrieves the root
named `"docs"`. To iterate through all the `ise` objects that are members of the `ises` set, the `foreach` DML command has been employed,
as shown below:

```
ise *p;
foreach (p, ises)
{
...
}
```

Queries that are used often can benefit from the addition of indexes. Indexes are special tables maintained by ObjectStore. In general,
indexes are b-trees or hash tables associated with a particular collection and element member. They reverse-map element member

values to elements. This allows for faster value-based tests and retrievals.

9.24 Relationships

In ObjectStore, it is possible to have one-way as well as two-way relationships between objects. ObjectStore supports the following types of relationships:

- 1:1
- 1:n
- n:1
- n:m

Bidirectional relationships can be used to ensure referential integrity. When the application code modifies one side of the relationship, ObjectStore automatically updates the other side to guarantee referential integrity. Thus, the programmer writes less code. Figure 9.6 highlights this issue.

If a health club offers two types of classes, Tae-Kwon-Do and Tai-Chi, and students are allowed to enroll in the classes, we can use two collections to represent the classes. In the diagram, Jim, Larry, Curly, and Moe are shown to be enrolled in the Tae-Kwon-Do class. If Moe decides to change classes and join the Tai-Chi class instead, the program code can update Moe's class attribute as shown below:

```
Moe.class = Tai_Chi;
```

The ObjectStore relationship facility automatically and transparently updates the collections representing the Tae-Kwon-Do and Tai-Chi classes to reflect this change. This might involve operations such as those indicated below:

```
Tae_Kwon_Do.remove("Moe");

Tai_Chi.insert("Moe");
```

The application developer has to indicate which members of an application's class form part of relationships. In ObjectStore, relationships are implemented by a special embedded relationship class that is transparent to the user. This embedded class intercepts access to relationships and updates them, and also ensures that the other end of the relationship is maintained. It is possible for application developers to implement custom relationship behavior by specializing ObjectStore relationship classes.

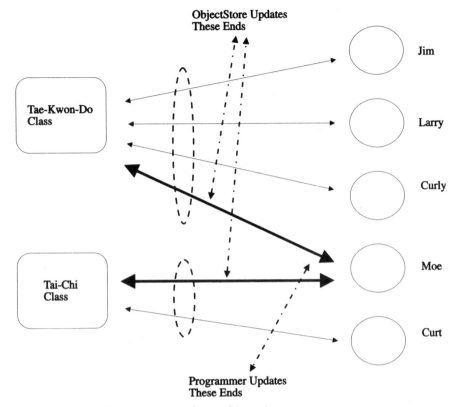

Figure 9.6 Relationships: ensuring referential integrity.

9.25 Version Management

When dealing with projects that need cooperative effort from several colleagues, locking a design document or software project for exclusive access would prove inconvenient. If coworkers are likely to spend several hours or days working on the same document or design, they could get their own copies of it and work on it, eventually creating their own versions. If the changes are not incompatible, it will be straightforward to merge the multiple versions some time later. Incompatible changes make merging versions later into a complex task.

If some component of a design is being worked on cooperatively, designers must be able to work on their own versions rather than being forced to wait for long periods until the lock on the component is released. In typical work environments, there is a need for configuration management facilities that allow different states of a design to be recorded and that allow alternative designs to be simultaneously available. ObjectStore's version management facilities provide support for cooperative work. The use of versions also necessitates the recording of relationships among various components of a design or document.

ObjectStore's version management facility provides support for the creation and manipulation of design versions and alternatives. It provides transparent support for relationships between components. The ObjectStore version facility makes use of two fundamental concepts in version management:

Configurations: Configurations serve as groupings of components and objects for the purpose of versioning. They serve as units of locking and versioning. The number of objects included in a configuration determines the granularity of the locking and versioning. It is possible to form subconfigurations.

Workspaces: Workspaces provide contexts for both shared and private work. The work done by a worker is always in the context of a workspace. Starting from a default workspace, child workspaces can be created where all current work is done. Thus, "work in progress" is contained in child workspaces, which inherit public shared data from parent or default workspaces.

9.26   Checkout and Checkin

A configuration is locked by checking it out of the current workspace's parent. Checkout is used to create a new version of the configuration. Configurations are checked out for modifications, and objects in parent workspaces need not be checked out in a child workspace for read-only access. After a configuration is created in a workspace, it can be checked in to the workspace's parent without a corresponding checkout.

Checking in a configuration replaces the old one. A version history of configurations is maintained, and old configurations are available as part of the version history. Versioning is also possible in the current workspace by means of the new_version member function.

9.27   Workspaces

Workspaces are specific areas (or components) of design environments in which a user (or a group of users) can experiment with a private copy of objects stored in a private database while being able to access objects from one or several shared databases. Workspaces allow parallel development of designs that can be subsequently merged to form a union of the designs. Each individual workspace can control the design process.

User application transactions typically operate in a current workspace. If an object cannot be located in a workspace, the ObjectStore system will be able to retrieve it from a global shared database.

9.28 Branching

Alternative development branches of the same configuration can be created by multiple checkouts. To obtain a parallel copy of a configuration that has already been checked out, the second application would call `configuration::checkout_branch()`, which creates a new version of the configuration while creating a new branch. When branched versions are checked in, the configuration is checked in to the *alternative branch* in the parent's workspace.

Alternative branches normally have to be merged back together, and merging usually involves comparing the different versions. This also implies that simultaneous access to multiple branches should be possible. A new version can be created by merging two predecessor versions.

9.29 Summary of ODI/ObjectStore

ObjectStore provides direct, transparent access to persistent data from within C++ programs. Persistence in ObjectStore is "orthogonal" to type. ObjectStore helps implement single-level storage; i.e., the programs treat the ObjectStore data exactly as they treat C or C++ data structures in memory.

ObjectStore takes advantage of the native operating system's virtual memory management, using a technique called virtual memory mapping. When persistent data referenced in an application are not in memory, the resulting page fault is intercepted by ObjectStore, and the referenced data are dynamically paged into virtual memory from the ObjectStore database.

The ObjectStore file system is either a raw partition or a UNIX file. ObjectStore databases are located in these file systems. Databases in ObjectStore are given a pathname that is in the same form as a UNIX pathname, and are always rooted starting with a '/'. The namespace for ObjectStore directories and databases is usually site-wide.

Databases are made up of segments. Segments are variable-sized regions of memory and are used as a unit of transfer from persistent memory in the database to the program memory. Segments are in turn made up of pages.

Schema information is stored in each database. Schema are stored as persistent C++ objects and are generated at compile time for each application.

ObjectStore requires two demon processes to be running before any ObjectStore application can run—the ObjectStore Server and the ObjectStore Directory Manager. The Server manages access to the ObjectStore file system, and the Directory Manager maintains a site-wide or local hierarchy of ObjectStore directories. A Cache Manager is started automatically whenever an ObjectStore application is started.

ObjectStore also provides a Data Manipulation Language (DML), a debugger that is based on gdb, a schema designer, and a class browser. It also provides an associative access query facility.

ObjectStore provides comprehensive support for collaborative work, and provides several facilities for creating cooperative work groups. These include configurations, workspaces, and no-conflict concurrency control.

References

1. Object Design, Inc., *ObjectStore User Guide,* 1992.
2. Object Design, Inc., *Introduction to ObjectStore,* Version 1.6, March 1992.

10

Objectivity/DB

Introduction

This chapter is dedicated to exploring the features and capabilities of the Objectivity/DB OODBMS. The architecture of Objectivity/DB is explored in detail. Persistence in Objectivity/DB is by inheriting from persistent classes. Programming examples are provided to explore the C++ programming interface. The examples introduce the reader to the Objectivity/DB data definition language (DDL), the C++ class libraries, and the development environment.

10.1   The Objectivity/DB OODBMS

Objectivity/DB is a high-performance object-oriented database designed to be used in heterogenous environments for engineering and commercial applications. It combines the best concepts of object-oriented technology (OOT) with the full DBMS functionality required for real-world applications, such as concurrency, transactional support, security, and versioning.

10.2   Highlights of Objectivity/DB

Objectivity/DB has many important features designed to meet the requirements of complex applications such as those found in engineering and design systems. The goals of Objectivity/DB include the following two important ones:

1. Commitment to industry standards

2. Portability

The main features of Objectivity/DB are listed below to provide a brief introduction to the Objectivity/DB system:

1. Flexible data modeling, with full support for object-oriented features including encapsulation and inheritance

2. Support for distributed architecture

3. Support for heterogeneous environments

4. Support for multiuser access, with concurrency control and atomicity

5. Short and long transactions, two-phase commit

6. Support for versioning of objects

10.3   System Components

Application software written using the Objectivity/DB programming interface makes use of some of the following system components (see Fig. 10.1):

1. Object Manager: It keeps track of and manipulates objects within the database. It also handles propagation and versioning.

2. Type Manager: It is responsible for storing, retrieving, and maintaining descriptions of all classes defined in the database.

3. Lock Manager: It oversees access to objects in the database and manages concurrent access to data.

4. Storage Manager: It is responsible for the physical placement of data in virtual memory and physical storage.

5. Network Manager: It coordinates communications between processes, allowing "local" processes to access data located on "remote" workstations.

10.4   Logical Storage Model

Objectivity/DB uses the following four logical storage entities:

- Basic Objects
- Container Objects
- Database Objects
- Federated Database Objects

10.5   Basic Objects

The fundamental unit of storage in Objectivity/DB is the *Basic Object*. A Basic Object belongs to a single Container Object. Each Basic Object within a Container has a scope name associated with that Container that uniquely identifies the object.

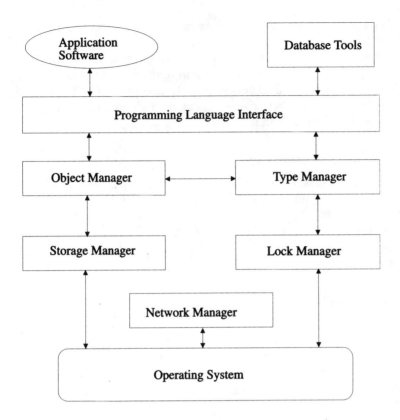

Figure 10.1   Objectivity/DB system components.

10.6   Container Objects

Container Objects may hold zero or more Basic Objects. Each Container Object belongs to a single Database Object. To improve performance, Basic Objects are physically clustered in a Container Object. Each Basic Object belongs to only one container in the database. A Basic Object in a container can be linked by "association" to other objects in other containers.

A container is an efficient way to access multiple Basic Objects. A database operation applied to a Container Object is applied to all Basic Objects it contains.

10.7   Database Objects

A Database Object consists of a *default Container Object* and one or more user-defined Container Objects. Users have the option of placing Basic Objects in user-defined Container Objects or letting the system place them in the default Container Object. Applications can simultaneously open and manipulate Basic Objects from multiple Container Objects, which may be located in multiple Database Objects on the network. Database Objects are part of a Federated Database Object. All Database Objects in a Federated Database Object share the same schema.

10.8   Federated Database Objects

A federated Database Object consists of a System Database Object and zero or more user-defined Database Objects (see Fig. 10.2). System Database Objects are automatically created when a Federated Database Object is created. A System Database Object contains the information necessary to maintain and administer the Federated Database Object.

10.9   Object Identifiers

Persistent objects in Objectivity/DB are given a unique object identifier (OID). OIDs are independent of the state of the objects. OIDs are used to locate and manage objects. An OID is constant during the lifetime of an object, and it helps identify the Database Object and the Container Object in which the object is located. OIDs can be used to compare object equivalence.

10.10   Persistent Classes and Persistent Objects in Objectivity/DB

Persistent objects are those that retain all their object properties beyond the scope of program execution. In Objectivity/DB, for an object to exist in the database, it must be an instance of a persistent class. A persistent class can be created by defining it as a subclass of one of the system-defined persistent classes. Thus, persistence is a property inherited from a persistent base class.

The class ooObj embodies persistence and serves as a base class from which other user-defined and system-defined classes become persistent. System-defined persistent classes are classes derived from class ooObj, such as

```
ooContObj
ooDBObj
```

The class element, shown below, is derived from a persistent base class ooObj, and thus becomes persistent. The class ooVString is used to create persistent strings. The class element has two data

Federated Database Object

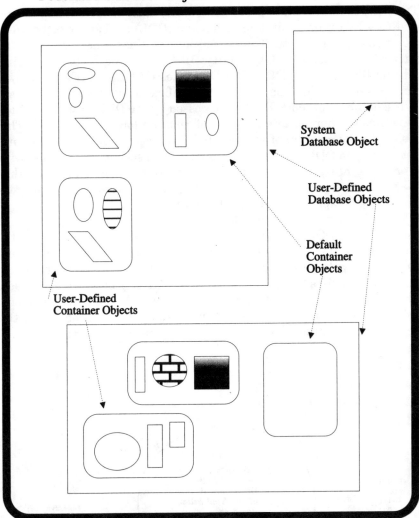

Figure 10.2 Objectivity/DB: logical storage model.

members, a string data member `text` and another string data member `element_id` to hold the name of `text`.

```
class element : public ooObj{
     ooVString text;
     ooVString element_id;
   public:
     int setelement(ooVString &str){text = str; return 0;};
     element(ooVString &str) { text = str;};
     int getelement(ooVString & str){str = text; return 0;};
};
```

10.11 The DDL File

The class structure of the persistent objects must be specified by means of a C++-like Data Definition Language (DDL) so that Objectivity/DB can create such objects. Thus, user-defined classes are presented as part of the schema to Objectivity/DB by creating a corresponding schema file using the DDL. The DDL uses C++ class declaration syntax, with minor additions to support specification of persistent objects.

The database schema files are processed by the DDL processor, which generates the appropriate schema information for Objectivity/DB. This results in the creation of a Federated Database Object if one does not yet exist. The DDL processor also generates a schema header file, with C or C++ syntax, which is then included in application programs so that they can access user-defined classes. Figure 10.3 highlights the process of creating an application using Objectivity/DB.

The document store example, which was previously dealt with in the chapter on ObjectStore, is revisited in this chapter. To recapitulate, *information source elements,* `ise,` have references to, or are associated with, document objects, `docobj`. A document object, `docobj`, consists of several elements that can be stored in a set. Thus, `docobj` has a reference to a set which contains `element` objects. The schema for the document store application consists of the declaration of classes `element`, `docobj`, and `ise` (see Fig. 10.4)

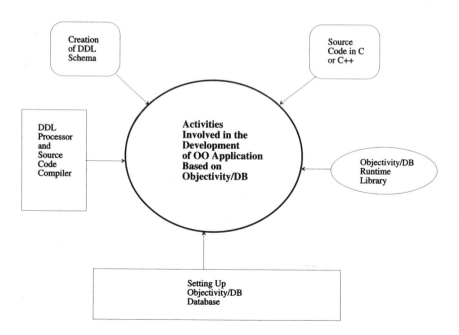

Figure 10.3 Activities involved in creating an application.

```
/*
*       doc.ddl : This is the declaration of relevant classes.
*/

#include "ooString.h"

class docobj: public ooObj{
  public:
    ooRef(ooContObj) cont_R;
    docobj(ooHandle(ooDBObj)), ooVString, ooVString);
    getElement(ooVString);
    putElement(ooVString);
};

class ise: public ooObj{
  public:
    ooVString name;
    ooVString status;
    ooHandle(docobj) bodyH;
    ise(ooHandle(ooDBObj) handle, ooVString filename,
      ooVString);
};
class element : public ooObj{
    ooVString text;
    ooVString element_id;
  public:
    int setelement(ooVString &str){text = str; return 0;};
    element(ooVString &str) { text = str;};
    int getelement(ooVString & str){str = text; return 0;};
};
```

In the schema definition above, the class ooObj is a persistent
base class which makes all three classes, docobj, ise, and element,
persistent.

10.12   Handles and References to Objects

Persistent objects can be accessed by means of handles or pointers. A
handle can access only one persistent object at a time. Handles are
declared as follows:

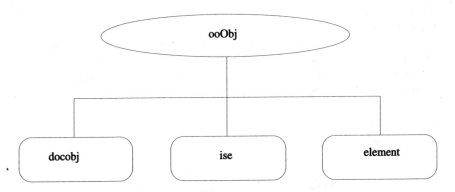

Figure 10.4   Persistence through inheritance.

```
ooHandle(docobj) bodyH;
```

This declares `bodyH` as a handle to an object instance of class `docobj`. References are also used for accessing persistent data, as shown below:

```
ooRef(ooContObj) cont_R;
```

This declares `cont_R` to be a reference to an instance of class `ooContObj`. As these examples indicate, the C++ interface to Objectivity/DB enforces strong type checking on objects.

The Federated Database bootstrap file

Each Federated Database is given a name and is located in a specific server. The Objectivity/DB lock server is also initiated on some workstation. The page size of the databases in the Federated Database has to be set to some specific size. All such information is specified in the Federated Database bootstrap file, as shown below:

```
ooFDDBFileName = first.FDDB
ooLockServerName = apollo
ooPageSize = 8192
ooFDNumber = 1234
```

The `ooFDNumber` is set to a unique number for each Federated Database.

10.13   Associations

An association is a construct that logically links objects. Associations can be binary. An association link is defined in each object's class so that objects can be made interdependent. Each association link is typed, indicating the persistent class it is compatible with.

Associations can be unidirectional or bidirectional. If bidirectional associations are used, it is possible to locate an associated object from either of the two associated objects. For example, in Fig. 10.5, each of the objects can locate the other.

The *cardinality* of an association refers to the number of objects on either end of the association. The cardinality of an association has to be specified when a class association link is specified. Objectivity/DB supports the following types of associations:

- 1:1 one-to-one
- 1:m one-to-many
- m:1 many-to-one
- n:m many-to-many

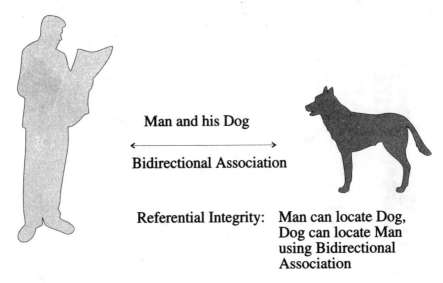

Man and his Dog

←——————————————→

Bidirectional Association

Referential Integrity: Man can locate Dog,
Dog can locate Man
using Bidirectional
Association

Figure 10.5   Bidirectional associations.

Figure 10.5 indicates a one-to-one bidirectional association between a man and his dog. A one-to-one bidirectional association allows a single instance of a class to be associated with a single instance of another class. Thus, in Fig. 10.5, a man (instance of the class of men) is allowed an association with a single dog (an instance of the class of canines). An example of a one-to-many association is the association between an employer and his employees. The relationship between instructors in a college and their students provides an example of a many-to-many bidirectional association. An instructor can have several students enrolled in a class, and a student can attend several classes, thus having several instructors. Figure 10.6 depicts this association.

10.14   Composite Objects Using Associations

If multiple objects are to be treated as one object, composite objects are the logical objects, and associations are the means to connect the objects. Composite objects can be constructed from simpler component objects using associations. An operation on a composite object may propagate to all of its associated objects. Propagation of operations along an association is optional, and is explicitly specified with the propagate attribute. Only the *delete, lock,* and *unlock* operations can be propagated.

Many-To-Many Bidirectional Associations

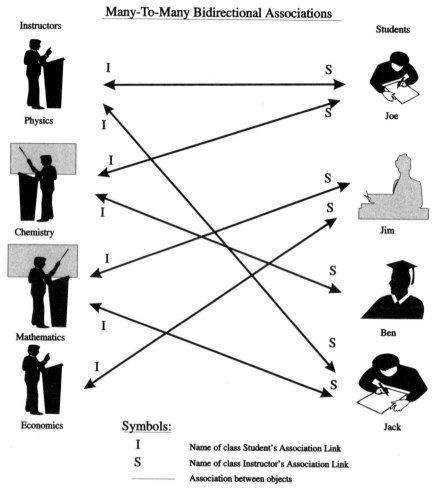

Figure 10.6 Many-to-many bidirectional associations.

10.15 The Scope Names and System Names

Objectivity/DB provides the facility of name spaces. It supports the following two concepts:

- System name space
- Scope name space

A system name space given to an object uniquely identifies an individual persistent object to Objectivity/DB. The Federated Database Object, Database Object, or Container Object can be given a name in the system name space. An object can have only one system name.

Federated Database Objects and Database Objects are given system names. System names are optional for Container Objects. System names for objects cannot be changed after they are assigned.

Scope names are based on the concept of *name scopes*. A name scope is an object's view of its environment and the name by which it knows other objects it interacts with. Only Container Objects and Basic Objects can have scope names. Each Basic or Container Object can have a single name within a given name scope. Scope names are typically strings.

10.16 Propagation of Operations through Associations

Operations on an object can be propagated to other objects with which the object is associated. The operations that can be propagated in Objectivity/DB are delete, lock, and unlock. Propagation along an association is optional, and is possible only when the operation is explicitly specified with the propagate attribute. Figure 10.7 depicts an example in which operations are propagated from object A to object E, although A and E are in different containers.

10.17 Propagation in Basic Objects and Containers

Container Objects are a basic structure in Objectivity/DB. Containers can contain several Basic Objects. In Fig. 10.7, container Cont1 con-

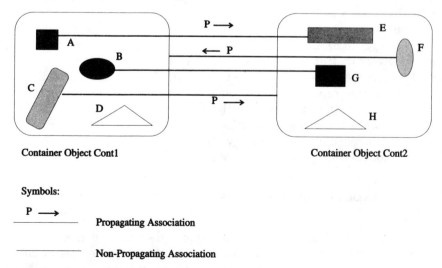

Container Object Cont1   Container Object Cont2

Symbols:

P ⟶
———————————— Propagating Association

———————————— Non-Propagating Association

Figure 10.7 Propagation in Basic Objects and Containers.

tains four basic objects, A, B, C, and D. Basic Object A has a propagating operation with Basic Object E in another container. A Container Object can be associated with Basic Objects in another container. A Container Object may also have associations with any other Container or Basic Object, both propagating and nonpropagating.

Database operations applied to a Container Object are also automatically applied to any Basic Objects it contains. Such operations are not allowed to propagate along the associations of the contained Basic Objects unless the operation is issued with the propagate attribute. In Fig. 10.7, the delete operation applied to Container Object Cont1 without propagation results in the deletion of only Container Cont1 and its Basic Objects, A, B, C, and D. Again, if the delete operation is applied with propagation to Container Cont1, it is deleted along with its own Basic Objects A, B, C, D, and the other basic objects with which they are associated, namely Basic Object E in Container Cont2.

If Container Object Cont2 is deleted with propagation, both Containers Cont1 and Cont2 get deleted, along with all the Basic Objects they contain. This is because Basic Object F in Cont2 has a propagating association with Container Object Cont1.

10.18   Versioning

Basic Objects in Objectivity/DB can be versioned. Several versions of the same Basic Object can be created. Objectivity/DB not only treats each version of a Basic Object as an independent persistent Basic Object, but also tracks each version as a particular version of the specific Basic Object.

Objectivity/DB supports both linear versioning and branch versioning (see Fig. 10.8). Linear versioning makes it possible to create a single new version from a Basic Object. Branch versioning makes it possible to create an arbitrary number of versions of the same Basic Object. *Version genealogy* is the term used to refer to the collection of and relationship between all versions of a Basic Object. Objectivity/DB provides facilities to specify a default version of a Basic Object from its genealogy. It also provides mechanisms to quickly locate the default version of an object.

10.19   The Document Store Example
Revisited

A version of the document store example is described in this section. The information source element objects are stored in the default con-

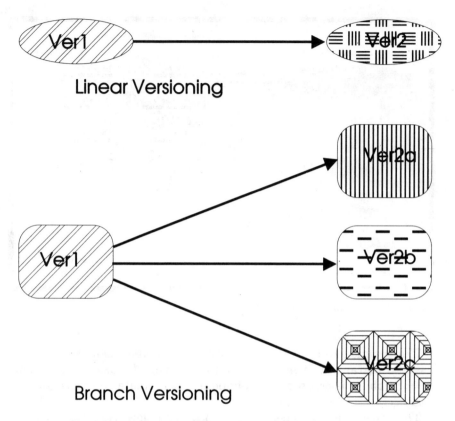

Figure 10.8   Versioning in Objectivity/DB.

tainer of an Objectivity/DB database. The Federated Database is first opened and a database is created so as to store the documents in the database. The organization of the database and the documents is shown in Fig. 10.9.

The constructor for the class of information source elements, ise, is as shown below:

```
/*
 *   ise.C : Definition of the ise class member functions
 */
#include <oo.h>
#include <ooString.h>
#include "doc.h" //User DDL schema header file
                 // Creating the object from file
ise::ise(ooHandle(ooDBObj) handle, ooVString filename,
         ooVString oidvar)
{
  set_bodyH(new(handle) docobj(handle, filename, oidvar));
}
```

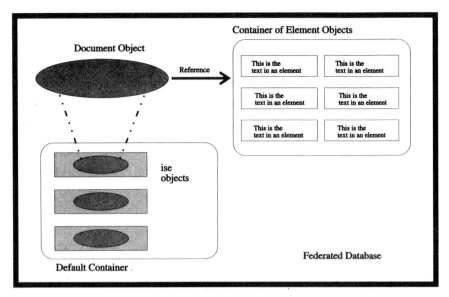

Figure 10.9   Organization of the database.

The function `set_bodyH` is a system-generated member function used to instantiate the `bodyH` data member of class `ise`. A new `docobj` object is created, and a handle to it is created and assigned to `bodyH`.

The constructor of class `docobj` is listed below. Notice the use of `ooNewCont` for creating a Container Object.

```
cont_R = ooNewCont(ooContObj, (), DBhandle, oidvar, 1, 3, 0);

/*
 *      docobj.C: Definition of the docobj class member functions
 */

#include <oo.h>
#include <ooString.h>
#include <stdlib.h>
#include <stdio.h>
#include "doc.h" //User DDL schema header file

docobj::docobj(ooHandle(ooDBObj) DBhandle,
               ooVString filename, ooVString oidvar)
{
   const MAX_LINE_LEN = 300;
   ooVString buffer;
   char str[MAX_LINE_LEN + 1];

   cont_R = ooNewCont(ooContObj, (), DBhandle, oidvar, 1, 3, 0);

   // Now parse the text in the file, and insert
   // segments into container.
```

```
char strvar[60], intstr[20];

FILE *fd;
               // Read from file
if ((fd = fopen(filename, "r")) = = NULL)
{
   fprintf(stderr, "Can't open %s in docobj()\n", filename);
   return;
}
          // Dummy parser: The following block of code simulates
          // the parsing of a document into its constituent segments.
          // These segments are encapsulated in element objects.
for (int segments = 0; segments < 20; segments++)
{
   buffer = "";
   for (int i = 0; i<10; i++)
   {
      if (fgets(str /*.head()*/, MAX_LINE_LEN, fd))
         buffer += str;
   }
          // Create scope names
   strcpy(strvar, "segid");
   sprintf(intstr, "%d", segments);
   strcat(strvar, intstr);

   ooHandle(ooContObj) cont_H = cont_R;

   ooHandle(element) el = new(cont_H) element(buffer);
          // Provide a Scope Name to the ise object.
   el.nameObj(cont_H, strvar);
}
fclose(fd);
}
```

Each `element` **object within the Container Object** `cont_H` **has a scope name unique to that Container Object.**

```
el.nameObj(cont_H, strvar);
```

The `nameObj()` **method takes a handle to the scope object and a pointer to a character string as parameters. In the code above, the element objects are given scope names which are created by concatenating the number of the segment of text to the string** `"segid"`.

The following program shows how databases can be created in Objectivity/DB.

```
/*
 *     doc_creat.C: Creates a new doc in the databases
 *     for Document source.
 *
 */

#include <oo.h> // Objectivity/DB system header file
#include <ooSchema.h> // Objectivity/DB system header file
#include "doc.h" // User DDL schema header file
#include <string.h>
#include <stream.h>
#include <iostream.h>
#include <stdio.h>
```

```
#include <stdlib.h>

main( int argc, char** argv)
{
  int start_num, end_num;
  char oidvar[30];

  if (argc < 7)
  {
    fprintf(stderr,
    "Usage: %s db_num input_filename start_doc No_docs outfile \n",
    argv[0]);
    exit(1);
  }

  int db_num = atoi(argv[1]);
  ooVString filename = argv[2];
  int start_doc = atoi(argv[3]);
  int ndocs = atoi(argv[4]);
  ooVString ofile = argv[5];

/////////////////////////////////////////////////////////////
//
// Initialize Objectivity/DB
//
/////////////////////////////////////////////////////////////

  ooInit(12, 200, 1000);

  filebuf outbuf;
  if (outbuf.open(ofile, output) = = 0)
  {
    cerr << "Cannot open output file \n";
    exit (1);
  }

  ostream outfile(&outbuf);

  const char *source = "DOC_SRC_";
  char doc_source[60], intstr[20];

  outfile << "Starting creation/population of docs:"
    << time(0) << "\n";
  outfile.flush();

  /* Start Transaction */
    ooRunStatus();
    ooTrans transaction;
    transaction.start();

    // Open the Federated Database

  ooHandle(ooFDObj) federatedDBH;
  if (federatedDBH.open("fed_objy", oocUpdate) ! = oocSuccess)
  {
    fprintf(stderr,
      "ERROR: Cannot open fed_objy Federated Database.\n");
    transaction.abort();
    exit(1);
  }

    /* creating Document source (Database) names */
  strcpy(doc_source, source);
```

```
    sprintf(intstr, "%d", db_num);
    strcat(doc_source, intstr);
    puts(doc_source);

    ooHandle(ooDBObj) databasedoc;
    if(databasedoc.open(federatedDBH, doc_source, oocUpdate)
       != oocSuccess)
    {
        fprintf(stderr, "ERROR: Cannot open docsource Database.\n");
        transaction.abort();
        exit(1);
    }

    /* create the documents, and store in database */

    for (int j = start_doc; j < start_doc + ndocs; j++)
    {
        strcpy(oidvar, "oid");
        sprintf(intstr, "%d", j);
        strcat(oidvar, intstr);
        puts(oidvar);
          // Create the ise in the default container of
          // the databasedoc database object.
        ooHandle(ise) ise_h =
          ooNew(ise, (databasedoc, filename, oidvar), databasedoc);

          // Provide a Scope Name to the ise object.
        ise_h.nameObj(databasedoc, oidvar);

        outfile << "Populated database: Document source: ise: "
                << doc_source << ":"
                << oidvar << " : "
                << time(0) << "\n";
        outfile.flush();

        if(databasedoc.close() != oocSuccess)
        {
            fprintf(stderr, "ERROR: Cannot close docsource Database.\n");
            transaction.abort();
            exit(1);
        }

        /* End Transaction, commit */
        transaction.commit();

    outfile << "End of creation/population of docs :"
            << time(0) << "\n";
    outfile.flush();

    // Exit
    exit(0);
}
```

10.20 Creating Multiple Databases in a Federated Database

There are several interesting ways by which the document store database could be created. In this section, we provide a second approach to creating the database, with the additional task of creating a whole set of databases. In fact, the following code attempts to create a set of

500 document store databases, all within the same Federated Database. The Federated Database is opened each time for each database. After populating each database, the Federated Database is closed and the transaction is committed.

```
/*
* creat.C: Creates the databases for Document sources
* After each database is created, commit each time in the loop.
*
*/

#include <oo.h> // Objectivity/DB system header file
#include <ooSchema.h> // Objectivity/DB system header file
#include "doc.h" // User DDL schema header file
#include <string.h>
#include <stream.h>
#include <iostream.h>
#include <stdio.h>
#include <stdlib.h>

main( int argc, char** argv)
{
  int start_num, end_num;
  char oidvar[30];
  if (argc < 7)
  {
    fprintf(stderr, "Usage: %s start_num end_num host path
input_filename No_docs outfile \n",
            argv[0]);
    exit(1);
  }

  start_num = atoi(argv[1]);
  end_num = atoi(argv[2]);
  ooVString host = argv[3];
  ooVString path = argv[4];
  ooVString filename = argv[5];
  int ndocs = atoi(argv[6]);
  ooVString ofile = argv[7];

    // Initialize Objectivity/DB
  ooInit(12, 200, 1000);

  filebuf outbuf;
  if (outbuf.open(ofile, output) = = 0) {
    cerr << "Cannot open output file \n";
    exit (1);
  }
  ostream outfile(&outbuf);

  const char *source = "DOC_SRC_";
  char doc_source[60], intstr[20];

  outfile << "Starting creation/population of Document sources:"
    << time(0) << "\n";
  outfile.flush();

  for (int i = start_num; i < end_num; i++)
  {
    ooRunStatus();
```

```
ooTrans transaction;
/* Start Transaction */
transaction.start();

  // Open the Federated Database
ooHandle(ooFDObj) federatedDBH;.
if (federatedDBH.open("fed_objy", oocUpdate) != oocSuccess)
{
  fprintf(stderr,
    "ERROR: Cannot open fed_objy Federated Database.\n");
  transaction.abort();
  exit(1);
}

/* creating Document source names */
strcpy(doc_source, source);
sprintf(intstr, "%d", i);
strcat(doc_source, intstr);
puts(doc_source); // message to user

ooHandle(ooDBObj) databasedoc = ooReplace(ooDBObj,
  (doc_source, 10,10, host, path), federatedDBH);

/* create the documents, and store in database */

for (int j = 0; j < ndocs; j++)
{
  strcpy(oidvar, "oid");
  sprintf(intstr, "%d", j);
  strcat(oidvar, intstr);
  puts(oidvar);
    // Create the ise in the default container of
    // the databasedoc database object.
  ooHandle(ise) ise_h =
    ooNew(ise, (databasedoc, filename, oidvar), databasedoc);
    // Provide a Scope Name to the ise object.
  ise_h.nameObj(databasedoc, oidvar);
  outfile << "Populated database: Document source: ise: "
    << doc_source << ":"
    << oidvar << " : "
    << time(0) << "\n";
  outfile.flush();
}

if(databasedoc.close() != oocSuccess)
{
  fprintf(stderr, "ERROR: Cannot close docsource Database.\n");
  transaction.abort();
  exit(1);
}

/* End Transaction, commit */
transaction.commit();
}
outfile << "End of creation/population of Document sources:"
  << time(0) << "\n";

exit(0); // Exit
}
```

In the example above, the Federated Database with the name fed_objy is opened. The database names are created by concatenating a number to the prefix DOC_SRC_. The ise objects are given scope names by concatenating the word "oid" with an ise number.

10.21 Accessing Document Elements from the Database

To access the element objects from the document store databases, it is necessary to know the scope name of the element object in the scope of the container of element objects. The reference to the container of element objects is available in the corresponding docobj object. To get to a specific docobj object, it is necessary to access the ise object that the document is associated with. A specific ise object can be accessed by means of the scope name of the object in the default container of the database. Thus, to get to a text element, these steps have to be followed:

1. Identify the specific ise object.

2. Access the ise object, and obtain access to the docobj object.

3. The docobj provides the reference to the container of element objects.

4. Identify the scope name of the element in the Container Object.

5. Access the element using the scope name.

```
/*
 *      axs_doc.C: Access documents (containers) from one
 *                 single doc (database). Extract the same
 *                 element (section of a document) from all
 *                 the ise objects.
 *
 */

#include <oo.h> // Objectivity/DB system header file
#include <ooSchema.h> // Objectivity/DB system header file
#include "doc.h" // User DDL schema header file
#include <string.h>
#include <stream.h>
#include <iostream.h>
#include <stdio.h>
#include <stdlib.h>

main( int argc, char** argv)
{
   int docdb_num, seg_num, num_docs;
   char oidvar[30], intstr[20];

   if (argc < 4) {
     fprintf(stderr, "Usage: %s docdb_num seg num_docs outfile \n",
             argv[0]);
     exit(1);
   }
```

```
    docdb_num = atoi(argv[1]); // database
    seg_num = atoi(argv[2]); // The text segment.
    num_docs = atoi(argv[3]);
    ooVString ofile = argv[4];
    char segvar[20];
    strcpy(segvar, "segid");
    sprintf(intstr, "%d", seg_num);
    strcat(segvar, intstr);

/////////////////////////////////////////////////////////
//
// Initialize Objectivity/DB
//
/////////////////////////////////////////////////////////

    /* Simultaneous opened files - max 12, Initial cache size
       of 200, max cache size of 1000 */
    ooInit(12, 200, 1000);

    filebuf outbuf;
    if (outbuf.open(ofile, output) = = 0)
    {
      cerr << "Cannot open output file \n";
      exit (1);
    }
    ostream outfile(&outbuf);

    const char *source = "DOC_SRC_";
    char doc_source[60];
    ooTrans transaction;
    transaction.start(); // Start transaction

    // Open the Federated Database
    ooHandle(ooFDObj) federatedDBH;
    if (federatedDBH.open("eval_objy", oocUpdate) ! = oocSuccess)
    {
      fprintf(stderr,
      "ERROR: Cannot open eval_objy Federated Database.\n");
      transaction.abort();
      exit(1);
    }

    /* creating Document source name */
    strcpy(doc_source, source);
    sprintf(intstr, "%d", docdb_num);
    strcat(doc_source, intstr);
    puts(doc_source);

    ooHandle(ooDBObj) databasedoc;
                  // Open the database in the Federated database
    if(databasedoc.open(federatedDBH, doc_source, oocUpdate)
      ! = oocSuccess)
    {
      fprintf(stderr, "ERROR: Cannot open docsource Database.\n");
      transaction.abort();
      exit(1);
    }

    outfile << "accessing the docs in a Document source:"
      << time(0) << "\n";
    outfile.flush();
```

```
for (int i = 0; i < num_docs; i++) // Access element num_docs times
{
  if (i == 100) // To check on the system status
    ooRunStatus();

      /* access the documents in the database */
  strcpy(oidvar, "oid");
  sprintf(intstr, "%d", i);
  strcat(oidvar, intstr);
  puts(oidvar); // message on user's screen
    // ise is in the default container of
    // the databasedoc database object.
  ooHandle(ise) ise_h;
  if (ise_h.lookupObj(databasedoc, oidvar) != oocSuccess)
  {
    fprintf(stderr,
        "ERROR: ise '%s' does not exist .\n", oidvar);
    transaction.abort();
    exit(1);
  }

  outfile << "accessing database for ise:"
    << oidvar << " : "
    << time(0) << "\n";

  outfile.flush();
  ooHandle(ooContObj) cont_H;
  cont_H = (ise_h->bodyH())->cont_R;
  if( cont_H.open() != oocSuccess)
  {
    fprintf(stderr,
      "ERROR: ise '%s' does not exist .\n", oidvar);
    transaction.abort();
    exit(1);
  }

  ooHandle(element) el_H; // Create handle object, then lookup
  if(el_H.lookupObj(cont_H, segvar) != oocSuccess)
  {
    fprintf(stderr, "ERROR: ise '%s' does not exist .\n",
    oidvar);
    transaction.abort();
    exit(1);
  }
  ooVString elstr;
el_H->getelement(elstr); // Get the element text, the segment
  puts(elstr); // Output the string accessed
  outfile << "element accessed:" << segvar << " : "
    << time(0) << "\n";
}

outfile << "End of accessing the population of Document source:"
  << time(0) << "\n";
outfile.flush();
if(databasedoc.close() != oocSuccess)
{
  fprintf(stderr,
    "ERROR: Cannot close docsource Database.\n");
  transaction.abort();
  exit(1);
}
  /* End Transaction */
```

```
      transaction.commit();
      // Exit
    exit(0);
  }
```

10.22　Retrieving an Object by Name

In this example code, the element object is accessed using the
lookupObj() method. Objectivity/DB provides the lookupObj()
method, which can be used to retrieve an object by name.

```
    lookupObj(scopeHandle, objName);
```

where scopeHandle is the handle of the object used as name scope
and objName is the name of the object to look up within the specified
name scope.

10.23　Updating the Database after a Lookup

If an element object has to be updated, the following steps are necessary:

1. Open the federated database.

2. Open the database.

3. Access the ise object to get to the docobj object.

4. Access the container of elements.

5. Access the element and update it.

Steps 1 through 4 are similar to the tasks performed by the previous example. Only step 5 is new. However, for completeness of the
code, all the steps will be repeated in the following example.

```
/*
*        axs_upd.C: Access element from database, then get one
*                   element to process it.
*/

#include <oo.h> // Objectivity/DB system header file
#include <ooSchema.h> // Objectivity/DB system header file
#include "doc.h" // User DDL schema header file
#include <string.h>
#include <stream.h>
#include <iostream.h>
#include <stdio.h>
#include <stdlib.h>

main( int argc, char** argv)
{
  char oidvar[30];

  if (argc < 4)
  {
```

```
      fprintf(stderr, "Usage: %s docdb doc_num seg outfile\n",
              argv[0]);
      exit(1);
  }

  char trail[50], timestr[20];
  int docdb_num = atoi(argv[1]);
  int doc_num = atoi(argv[2]);
  int seg = atoi(argv[3]);
  strcpy(trail, argv[4]);

///////////////////////////////////////////////////////////
//
// Initialize Objectivity/DB
//
///////////////////////////////////////////////////////////

  ooInit(12, 1000, 1000);
  /* Start Transaction */
  ooTrans transaction;
  transaction.start();
  // Open the Federated Database for Update
  ooHandle(ooFDObj) federatedDBH;
  if (federatedDBH.open("fed_objy", oocUpdate) != oocSuccess)
  {
     fprintf(stderr, "ERROR: Cannot open fed_objy Federated
Database.\n");
     transaction.abort();
     exit(1);
  }

///////////////////////////////////////////////////////////
//
// Open the Database
//
///////////////////////////////////////////////////////////

  const char *source = "DOC_SRC_";
  char doc_source[60], intstr[20];

  strcpy(doc_source, source);
  sprintf(intstr, "%d", docdb_num);
  strcat(doc_source, intstr);
  puts(doc_source);

  ooHandle(ooDBObj) databasedoc;
  if(databasedoc.open(federatedDBH, doc_source, oocUpdate)
     != oocSuccess)
  {
     fprintf(stderr, "ERROR: Cannot open docsource Database.\n");
     transaction.abort();
     exit(1);
  }

     /* access the document in database */
  strcpy(oidvar, "oid");
  sprintf(intstr, "%d", doc_num);
  strcat(oidvar, intstr);
  puts(oidvar);
     // access the ise in the default container of
     // the databasedoc database object.
```

```
  ooHandle(ise) ise_h;
  if (ise_h.lookupObj(databasedoc, oidvar) != oocSuccess)
  {
    fprintf(stderr,
      "ERROR: ise '%s' does not exist.\n", oidvar);
    transaction.abort();
    exit(1);
  }
      // access the container where the element objects are stored
  ooHandle(ooContObj) cont_H;
  cont_H = (ise_h->bodyH())->cont_R;
  if( cont_H.open() != oocSuccess)
  {
    fprintf(stderr,
      "ERROR: container of element objects does not exist.\n");
    transaction.abort();
    exit(1);
  }
      // Create the name of the element object
  char segvar[20];
  strcpy(segvar, "segid");
  sprintf(intstr, "%d", seg);
  strcat(segvar, intstr);
  puts(segvar);
                // Access the element object
  ooHandle(element) el_H;
  if(el_H.lookupObj(cont_H, segvar) != oocSuccess)
  {
    fprintf(stderr,
      "ERROR: ise '%s' does not exist .\n", oidvar);
    transaction.abort();
    exit(1);
  }

  ooVString elstr;
  el_H->setelement(elstr); // Update the element object
  puts(elstr);

  if(databasedoc.close() != oocSuccess)
  {
    fprintf(stderr, "ERROR: Cannot close docsource Database.\n");
    transaction.abort();
    exit(1);
  }

///////////////////////////////////////////////////////////
//
// Shutdown Objectivity/DB
//
///////////////////////////////////////////////////////////

  federatedDBH.close(); // Close the Federated Database
  transaction.commit(); // Commit the transaction
  exit(0); // Exit
}
```

10.24 The ooMap Class

Objectivity/DB provides the class ooMap that can be used as a persistent base class to create derived classes that have the ability to pro-

vide faster and scalable access to the objects. The following class declaration indicates its usage:

```
class docobj: public ooMap
{
  public:
    ooHandle (ise) headerH <-> bodyH: inline(long), prop(delete);

    docobj(ooVString filename);
    getElement(ooVString);
    putElement(ooVString);
};
```

An inline association is added to connect the docobj instances with instances of class ise. This allows easy access either way—ise object used for query and browsing, and docobj used for direct access to the element objects in the document.

10.25   A Better DDL for the Document Store Database

In this section, bidirectional associations will be explored to allow direct access to the docobj object without sacrificing the ability to access the ise data. A revised DDL is shown below. The approach taken is as follows:

1. Use ooMap for speedy access to element objects.

2. Create containers in batch, instead of creating a container in the constructor of the docobj class.

3. The ise object is made responsible for creating and naming the docobj.

4. An inline association is added to docobj, so that access is easier in the bidirectional relationship.

```
/*
 *    doc2.ddl : This is an improved declaration of relevant classes.
 */

#include "ooString.h"
#include "ooMap.h"

class docobj: public ooMap{
  public:
    ooRef(ooContObj) cont_R;
    ooHandle (ise) headerH <-> bodyH : inline(long), prop(delete);
    docobj(ooVString filename);
    getElement(ooVString);
    putElement(ooVString);
};
```

```
class ise: public ooObj{
  public:
    ooVString name;
    ooVString status;
    ooHandle(docobj) bodyH <-> headerH: inline(long), prop(delete);
    ise(ooHandle(ooContObj) & containerHandle, ooVString filename,
      ooVString oidvar);
};

class element : public ooObj{
    ooVString text;
    ooVString element_id;
  public:
    int setelement(ooVString &str){text = str; return 0;};
    element(ooVString &str) { text = str;};
    int getelement(ooVString & str){str = text; return 0;};

};
```

In the DDL above, the `ise` object is made responsible for creating and naming the `docobj`. A batch container create can be employed. The `ise` constructor will name the `docobj` the same as the `oidvar`. The `ise` constructor is shown below:

```
ise::ise(ooHandle(ooContObj) & containerHandle, ooVString filename,
ooVString oidvar)
{
      // Provide cluster hint for docobj
    ooHandle(docobj) docobjHandle = new(containerHandle)
  docobj(filename);
    set_bodyH(docobjHandle);
      // Name the docobj in the scope of the database
    docobjHandle.nameObj(containerHandle.containedIn(), oidvar);
}
```

In the constructor for `ise`, when the `docobj` objects are created using the `new` method, a cluster hint is provided so that `docobj` objects get created in `containerHandle`. The container to store the elements of the `docobj` is, in this case, created in batches and passed in an argument to the `ise` constructor, as shown above. The revised constructor for the `docobj` class is as shown below.

```
/*
 *         docobj.C: Definition of the docobj class member functions
 */

#include <oo.h>
#include <ooString.h>
#include <stdlib.h>
#include <stdio.h>
#include "doc.h" //User DDL schema header file

docobj::docobj(ooVString filename)
        : ooMap(100, 2, 50) // Arguments to the ooMap constructor
  {
```

```
const MAX_LINE_LEN = 300;
ooVString buffer;
char str[MAX_LINE_LEN + 1];

// The container to store the elements of the docobj is, in this case,
// created in batches and passed in an argument to the ise
// constructor.
// Now parse the text in the file, and insert
// segments into container.

char strvar[60], intstr[20];
FILE *fd;
// Read from file
if ((fd = fopen(filename, "r")) = = NULL)
{
  fprintf(stderr, "Can't open %s in docobj()\n", filename);
  return;
}
    // Dummy parser: The following block of code simulates
    // the parsing of a document into its constituent segments.
    // These segments are encapsulated in element objects.
for (int segments = 0; segments < 20; segments++)
{
  buffer = "";
  for (int i = 0; i<10; i++)
  {
    if (fgets(str /*.head()*/, MAX_LINE_LEN, fd))
      buffer += str;
  }
        // Create scope names
  strcpy(strvar, "segid");
  sprintf(intstr, "%d", segments);
  strcat(strvar, intstr);

  ooHandle(element) el = new(ooThis()) element(buffer);
  // Instead of providing a scopename as before, provide an
  // ooMap dictionary name - docobj is subclass of ooMap
 add(strvar, el)

}
fclose(fd);
}
```

10.26   Summary of Objectivity/DB

Objectivity/DB envisions (and implements) a four-level hierarchy for
the storage model, and access to multiple, physically distributed databases is the goal. The four logical storage entities are Basic Objects,
Containers, Databases, and Federated Databases.

1. **Basic Objects:** This is the fundamental storage entity of
   Objectivity/DB. Basic Objects are logically stored in Containers.

2. **Containers:** A Container holds a collection of Basic Objects. To
   improve performance, the Basic Objects in a Container can be
   physically clustered in memory.

3. Databases: Every database has a default Container, and can contain several user-defined Containers. The default Container is used to house Basic Objects that are not explicitly placed in a user-defined container. An application can simultaneously open and manipulate Basic Objects in multiple Containers and multiple databases, which may be distributed on multiple network nodes.

4. Federated Databases: A Federated Database contains user-defined databases. All databases in a Federated Database share the same schema. Applications can create objects of classes defined in this schema.

In Objectivity/DB, persistence is provided by means of system-defined persistent classes like ooObj, ooContObj, and subclasses derived from them. To exist in a database, an object must be an instance of a persistent class.

Objectivity/DB also offers support for composite objects and associations. Composite objects are constructed from simpler objects using associations. Relationships between objects can be modeled using associations. Such associations are specified in the schema of persistent data.

Each association helps implement a typed link. The cardinality of the associations can be 1:1, 1:m, m:1, or n:m. An operation on a composite object can be made to propagate to all of its associated objects.

To access objects, Objectivity/DB provides the following features:

1. Handle, which is a nonpersistent object that serves as an interface between applications and persistent objects.

2. References, which provide a type-safe way to directly access objects of a specific class and its subclasses. They can be used as instance members.

3. Iterators, to obtain handles of objects. Iterators can be used to locate and navigate thorough a collection of objects.

Objectivity/DB facilitates versioning by allowing maintenance of multiple copies of the same Basic Object. The semantics of a new version are up to the application.

Reference

1. Objectivity, Inc., *Objectivity/DB System Overview*, Version 1.1, March 1991.

11

Versant

Introduction

In this chapter, the features of the Versant OODBMS will be explored. The Versant object model and the Versant architecture are briefly touched upon. The Versant Manager and the Versant Server are described in detail. Object management in Versant is also covered.

11.1 The Versant OODBMS

Versant is an object-oriented database system that is particularly useful when several teams work in parallel on different parts of a project, project requirements change over time, diverse activities must be tied together, a distributed environment is necessary, or complex data types are employed.

11.2 The Versant Object Model

Versant supports class-based object orientation. All objects have to belong to some class. Objects have identity. Each class and instance object in the object database has a unique identifier created by the database system when the object is created. This identifier is called the Logical Object Identifier (LOID). It is stored with the object and consists of a database identifier and an object identifier. When an object is deleted, its LOID is not recycled or reused. Thus, LOIDs are guaranteed to be unique, even across database boundaries. Dangling references to objects are not a problem, since LOIDs are never reused. LOIDs do not provide information on the actual storage locations of objects. The physical location of an object is stored in another identifi-

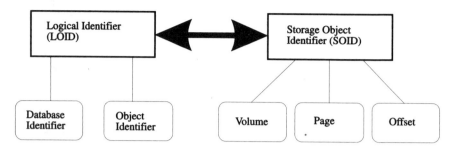

Figure 11.1 Versant object identifiers.

er called a Storage Object Identifier (SOID). It is composed of the following three numbers (see Fig. 11.1):

- Volume identifier
- Page number
- Offset

LOIDs have to be mapped into SOIDs before they can be brought into memory.

Objects can have relationships with other objects. The following are the types of relationships supported in Versant:

- Simple links
- Aggregate links
- Multiple links
- Embedded objects
- Single inheritance
- Multiple inheritance

A link is a reference or a pointer to an object. A link establishes a persistent, noninheritance, unidirectional relationship between two objects. Object links are good for performance. Unlike in relational tables, all linked objects are available when one object is retrieved, without the need to perform costly joins. Links can be considered to be a "hasA" relationship.

Embedded objects are useful to implement a nested structure, where the embedded object is an attribute whose type is a class or structure. Embedded objects can be an internal object, an embedded array of objects, or a embedded array of links.

A single inheritance relationship typically states that a derived class "is kind of" a base class, only more specialized. Multiple inheritance indicates that the derived class "is a" kind of two or more base classes.

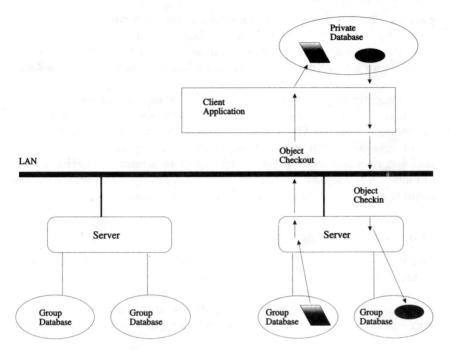

Figure 11.2   Versant architecture.

11.3   The Versant Architecture

Versant is designed to support a client/server approach to distributed
computing (see Fig. 11.2). Any number of client applications, server
processes, user workstations, and server machines may cooperate in a
Versant fully distributed database. The database can be set up as an
m-clients/n-servers system.

A *server* in the Versant environment is a machine that runs a server
process that supports concurrent access by multiple users to one or
more databases. A *client* is an application process that has access to a
private persistent database workspace and, in addition, can access several databases on servers concurrently with other client applications.

Users can have their own private database on a workstation. This
is sometimes referred to as private workspace. Their applications can
access their private databases as well as the shared databases on the
server machines. Users make use of checkin/checkout facilities to
work on subsets of objects without interference from other users
working on the same objects.

11.4   The Storage Architecture

The storage places on disk are called volumes. Each database can
have several volumes on disk. Volumes can be either files or raw

devices. Versant creates a system volume for each database automatically when the database is installed. The system volume is where all class descriptions are stored, in addition to object instances. Versant provides an add volume utility to add additional volumes to the database.

To keep track of transaction activities, a logical log volume and a physical log volume are necessary. Both volumes are created when a database is created. The Versant Manager maintains a memory cache for objects. When an object is requested by an application, the object cache is checked first to see if the object is already in cache. If the object is not located in the cache, the Versant Manager sends a request to the Versant Server to retrieve the object.

11.5 The Versant Manager

The Versant Manager (Fig. 11.3) is the database kernal that manages object definition and access. It is responsible for manipulating classes, handling queries, managing updates across database boundaries, object caching, and providing support for long transactions. When application programs need to begin a long transaction or commit

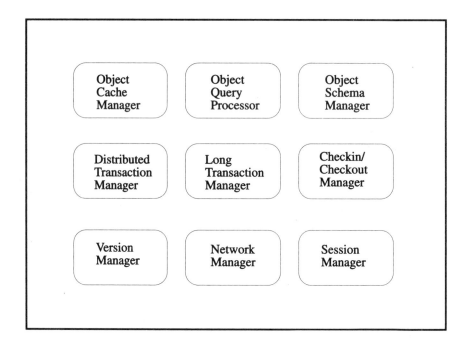

Figure 11.3 Versant manager.

changes to the database, they communicate with the Versant Manager using the language-specific interfaces. The Versant Manager, in turn, communicates with Versant Servers which manage the storage of object instances to secondary storage devices.

The Versant Manager has the following software components:

1. Object Schema Manager
2. Object Query Processor
3. Object Cache Manager
4. Distributed Transaction Manager
5. Version Manager
6. Long Transaction Manager
7. Network Manager
8. Checkin/Checkout Manager
9. Session Manager

Structurally, the Versant Manager is divided into two components:

1. The component that is associated with an application and an object cache
2. The component that is associated with a Versant Server and a server page cache.

11.6   The Versant Server

Each Versant Server accesses one database. The Versant Servers form a layer of software between the Versant Managers and the operating system layer that deals with retrieval and storage of data in database volumes. The Versant Manager communicates with the Versant Server which handles data storage and retrieval. Versant Servers are responsible for providing support for short transactions, lock objects, logging, and recovery. At the Server level, the system does not deal with objects.

When a user begins a session with a client application, he or she automatically uses both the Versant Manager and Versant Server. The Server and the Manager can be on the same machine or on different machines.

11.7   Persistence in Versant OODBMS

In Versant, in addition to data, locks and relationships can be made persistent. Any type of data can be stored in the database and managed using the database facilities. Versant provides the following categories of persistence:

1. Object persistence
2. Class persistence
3. Lock persistence
4. Structural persistence
5. Complex data persistence

Persistence, in Versant, is a property that is embodied in a class called `Persistent`. When a new class is created, if it has an inheritance path to the `Persistent` class in the Versant library, then its instances can be saved in the database and its class definitions will be saved as an instance of the `Class` class in the library file as well as in the database. When instances of that class are subsequently created, it is necessary to specify whether the instances should be permanent or transient, using the `Persistent` macro.

11.8   Object Management

The Versant Manager maintains a hash table, called the Object Cache Table, to keep track of objects in memory (see Fig. 11.4). The

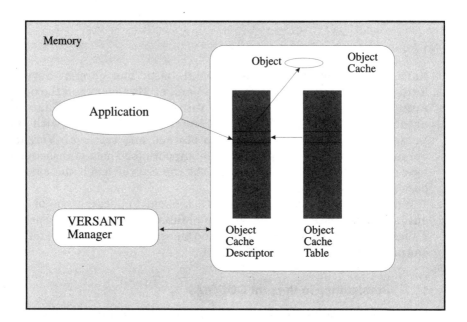

Figure 11.4   Object cache management.

Object Cache Table is keyed on LOIDs and contains memory pointers and information about the lock status of objects. Each active database has its own Object Cache Table.

Objects can be swapped in and out of cache memory. To account for object swapping, the Object Cache Table creates and maintains Cached Object Descriptors. Applications access the Cached Object Descriptors rather than the Object Cache Table or a pointer to the actual location of the object. The Cached Object Descriptors serve as an intermediate level of redirection and allow the Versant Manager to swap objects in and out of memory.

Only active transactions can access their Object Cache Table, and each entry in the table points to a Cached Object Descriptor, which in turn points to the actual object. If the Cached Object Descriptor points to null, then the object must be swapped into cache. Every transaction has its own cache, and copies of the same object can be residing in different caches of different transactions conducted by different applications.

When a transaction terminates, all modified or new objects from the cache are sent to their respective Versant Servers so that changes can be logged.

11.9   The Database Identifier

The database identifier file is maintained to keep track of the databases in a distributed system. All Server machines and client workstations in the network must be able to access this file. After the database identifier file is created at system installation, it is automatically updated whenever a new database is created in the network. There can be only one database identifier file in the distributed database network.

11.10   Transactions

Versant supports a wide range of transactional activities. It allows both short and long transactions. The transactions can terminate in different types of commits and rollbacks, which save or abandon changes. The transactions can take advantage of different types of object locks. For long transactions, checkouts are possible, which provide additional control over objects and allow manipulation of objects in a persistent, private database. In Versant, the following transaction-related activities are orthogonal in concept and application:

1. Short and long transactions
2. Short and long commits

3. Short and persistent locks

4. Checkouts

11.11   Short Transactions

A short transaction is the basic type of transaction, and an application is always in a short transaction by default. Client applications can be in only one short transaction at a time. When an application starts a session, it is put in a short transaction by default, and when the short transaction is terminated, another short transaction is automatically started. A short transaction can involve several databases. Versant allows savepoints within short transactions. Objects can be locked implicitly in a transaction. Objects can also be locked explicitly.

Short transactions do not survive system crashes. Short transactions can be named. Naming of transactions is a good idea, as it enables easier examination of the transactional logs in case of hardware failure.

When a short commit occurs, all database actions are made persistent and all short locks are released. Objects are dropped from cache memory. A new short transaction is automatically started. It is possible to perform short commits even with checked-out objects. For checked-out objects, changes to the objects are made persistent only to the personal or private database to which those objects have been checked out.

If it is necessary to transmit changes to the objects down to the database without having to release the locks on the objects, a checkpoint commit should be used. A checkpoint commit makes database actions persistent, retains short locks, and also keeps objects in cache memory.

A savepoint is a important feature that can be used to return the database to a consistent state in the event of a transaction failure, or by choice. A savepoint in a short transaction is a logical, conceptual snapshot of conditions and object values at a particular moment of time, to which it is possible to return by executing an undosavepoint command. A savepoint does not make changes to object values persistent. It only marks a point to which it is possible to return.

11.12   Long Transactions

Long transactions are typically associated with checkin/checkout facilities. They are used to provide transactional support for activities that span several sessions and processes, lasting for a long period of time. Long transactions make it possible to check out objects and work on them in several sessions over any length of time. If the private database to which objects were checked out crashes, persistent locks are maintained. During recovery, the long transactions are reconstructed and objects are restored to their state at the last short commit.

Both sessions and long transactions make use of short transactions. A long transaction is made up of one or more sessions. A session helps establish connection to databases, the first of which is typically the persistent workspace. In the current release of Versant, an application is always in a long transaction.

11.13   Commits and Rollbacks

A two-phase protocol is employed for short commits and checkpoint commits. This makes it possible to roll back or commit all changes to all databases in transactions that span multiple databases. This takes care of situations where some databases may be cut off from others in the network. Two-phase commits are also used for long transactions, and long commits will fail if there are outstanding checkouts. Checkouts can also be rolled back just like object changes. However, database activities like beginning a session or establishing database connections cannot be rolled back.

11.14   Locks

Locks are applied at the object level. In the case of embedded objects, locks are propagated to the embedded objects. There are two basic kinds of locks:

1. Short lock
2. Persistent lock

The main difference between them is the fact that persistent locks survive a system disruption, while short locks do not. Short locks do not survive the end of a short transaction, the end of a database session, or a system disruption. A persistent lock implies a short lock. It is possible to set short or persistent read or write locks. A read lock allows simultaneous reads from several processes. A write lock disables read or write accesses from other processes. There are four basic lock modes:

1. Null lock
2. Read lock
3. Update lock
4. Write lock

A null lock is not really a lock. It permits access to the object immediately regardless of other locks. An update lock guarantees the next write lock on an object. An update lock is similar to a read lock in that it allows other users to read the locked object but not update it.

If a short lock is placed on a class object, all accesses, whether read or write, to the class or instances of the class are prohibited. Subclasses and their instances are also inaccessible during the duration of the lock on a class object.

The behavior of locks is somewhat dependent upon the chosen language interface. The locking facilities for the C language interface differ slightly from those available to the C++ language interface.

11.15   Versioning

Objects in Versant can be versioned. Small objects as well as large objects can be versioned, and can have several versions. Each version of an object can have different status. The checkin/checkout mechanism is typically employed to create versions of objects in individual workspaces.

Keeping track of all the different versions of all objects is a complicated issue. The Versant database is responsible for version tracking. Versions are tracked in a version derivation graph. Versions can have

- Multiple parents
- Multiple children
- Multiple siblings

To keep track of all the versioned objects in an application, Versant provides the *configuration* facility. Configuration of versions is maintained even when versions evolve across database boundaries.

Versant can resolve version relationships at runtime with dynamic binding. One of the versions is a default version. Typically, the default version is the most recent version in the version derivation graph. It is also possible to explicitly set a particular version as the default version. It is sometimes necessary to merge versions, and Versant provides facilities for merging versions.

11.16   Process and Session Configurations

A *process* is a computing entity that uses computing resources. In Versant, a client process includes a client application and part of the Versant Manager. The server process on a server machine includes part of the Versant Manager and all of the Versant Server. Versant allows the creation of one or two processes as part of the client application. The process configuration alternatives are the following:[1]

1. Use one process for a client application, Versant Manager, and the Versant Server.

2. Use one process for a client application and part of the Versant Manager and another process for part of the Versant Manager and all of a Versant Server.

Applications can run with one or two processes depending upon which Versant library is linked with the applications. The library `libosc.a` is used for the single-process case, and the library `liboscfe.a` is used to specify two processes while linking the application program.

A database *session* is started to manipulate objects that are stored in the database. A session consists of a client process that communicates with a server process which is responsible for managing the objects in the database. After starting a session, the client process can establish links to as many group databases as it needs to. The client process and the server process can be executing on the same workstation.

A session must have access to a persistent database workspace to do the following:

1. Create objects
2. Perform two-phase commits
3. Serve as a default database

11.17   Versant in Distributed Environments

Versant allows multiple client applications to transparently access data distributed among multiple servers in a fully distributed database architecture. Application interfaces are available to all client applications. Using distributed transactions, it is possible to retrieve, add, edit, and remove data from multiple databases in a single transaction.

11.18   Capacity of Versant Database

A Versant database can hold up to a total of 2^{48} objects and classes. Versant is designed to support a large number of server machines and networks to provide a distributed database environment. The number of databases, servers, and workstations combined should not exceed 2^{16}. There is also a limit on the size of objects. The size of an object should not exceed 2^{32} bytes.

11.19   Interfaces to Versant OODBMS

Standard C and C++ can be used to access the data stored in Versant. Versant provides a set of development utilities which can be used to browse application schema and data. Versant also provides means to alter schema in the database. The C and C++ libraries provided with

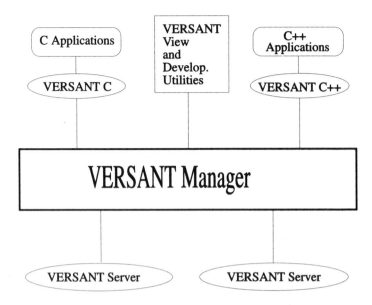

Figure 11.5 Software development in Versant.

the database contain functions and methods that manipulate the database, such as methods that begin a session, find and change objects, and perform commits. See Fig. 11.5).

11.20 Benefits of Using Versant

The following benefits can be derived from the Versant implementation of object databases:

1. Object persistence, object sharing, and object consistency with recovery from system crashes.
2. Ability to use complex data types. This makes it possible to use Versant for a large range of applications.
3. Standard C and C++ languages and environments are supported.
4. Ability to manipulate objects in persistent, personal workspaces.
5. Ability to migrate objects from personal workspaces to server machines.
6. Support of workgroup with database integrity due to concurrency, versioning, transaction control, and two-phase commits.
7. Distributed database architecture supported, with site autonomy.
8. Scalable performance.

9. Ability to involve any number of server machines and workstations in a distributed database system.

10. Caching and clustering possible for better performance.

11. Both short and long transactions supported.

12. Object model supports both single inheritance and multiple inheritance.

Reference

1. *VERSANT System Reference Manual,* Chapter 2, "System Details," VERSANT Version 1.7 for Sun Workstations, February 1992, pp. 2-14 to 2-15.

Evaluation of OODBMSs

Introduction

This chapter is dedicated to issues related to the evaluation of object-oriented database management systems (OODBMSs). Evaluation based on both technical and nontechnical issues are covered in this chapter. A major portion of this chapter focuses on the evaluation of different OODBMS features.

12.1 Evaluations of OODBMSs

It is important to test all critical aspects of OODBMSs before selecting one from the list of potential systems. In the absence of good benchmarks, it is important to design prototypes and test them for all the important criteria. It is important to critically examine and compare the various features available in all OODBMSs as part of a meaningful evaluation. A comparative objective rating scheme must be developed for the evaluations.

12.2 The Need for Prototypes

It is important to test the required OODBMS functionality thoroughly as part of the evaluations. To this end, it is good to build a prototype of the actual application and simulate the actual object access patterns.

Designing and testing a prototype serves two important purposes:

1. It provides a proof of the concept. It helps highlight potential problems with the design.

2. It serves as a testbed for performance evaluations. It makes the evaluations more realistic and makes the benchmarks more meaningful.

The evaluation prototypes must push the OODBMS to the limit as part of the evaluation. The following are some of the steps involved in designing and developing prototypes:

1. Identify the goals of the prototype effort.
2. Create the required number of evaluation prototype applications to simulate the normal operations in the application environment.
3. Create the data schema that represents the actual application. Create the required number of databases, containers, and other OODBMS structures to simulate the normal layout of the data in the application environment. This should be done as part of the evaluation of the "data population" process. The average time to create a database, container, or an object is calculated for comparisons to other OODBMSs.
4. Create special application prototypes to test random-access time for different kinds of objects from the OODBMS.

12.3   Issues to Be Considered

The issues that must be addressed during the evaluation of OODBMS can be broadly categorized into the following two categories:

Technical issues

Nontechnical issues

12.4   Technical Issues

The following are some of the technical issues that must be included in OODBMS evaluations. Researchers working on the DEC 007 benchmark for OODBMSs consider the items on this list to be the key determinants in OODBMSs.

1. Pointer traversal
2. Application-DBMS coupling
3. Complex object support
4. Updates
5. Recovery
6. Path indexing

7. Long data items

8. Clustering

9. Queries and optimization

10. Caching

11. Concurrency control

12. Relationships

13. Versioning

A more comprehensive list of evaluation criteria is provided below:

1. Atomicity of transactions

2. Consistency in transactions

3. Encapsulation and isolation of internal state of transactions

4. Durability of transactions

5. Long transactions

6. Nested transactions

7. Shared transactions

8. Nonblocking read consistency

9. Concurrency control issues

10. Lock escalation

11. Promotable locks

12. Locks set and release

13. Granularity of locks

14. Deadlock detection

15. Role assignment for security

16. Role authorization

17. Implicit role authorization

18. Positive and negative authorization

19. Strong and weak authorization

20. Authorization objects

21. Authorization by time and day

22. Multilevel security

23. Query language

24. Query optimization

25. Indexing

26. Queries in programs
27. Query language completeness
28. Specification of collections
29. SQL as a query language
30. Support for views
31. Schema modification
32. Update time
33. Changes to attributes
34. Addition of attributes to a class
35. Deleting attributes from a class
36. Changing the name of an attribute
37. Changing static members of a class
38. Adding new methods to a class
39. Dropping an existing class method
40. Changing the name of a method
41. Changing the inheritance of a method
42. Adding and removing a superclass to an existing class
43. Changes to an existing class
44. Versioning schema
45. Location independence in distributed database system
46. Local autonomy at each site
47. Fragmentation and replication independence
48. Distributed query processing
49. Distributed transaction processing
50. Hardware independence
51. Operating system and network independence
52. Object model
53. Dynamic binding and polymorphism
54. Encapsulation
55. Object identity
56. Types and classes
57. Inheritance and delegation
58. Relationship and attributes

59. Literal data types
60. Multimedia objects
61. Aggregate objects
62. Composite and complex objects
63. Integrity
64. Schema extensibility
65. Extensibility of database operations
66. Language for object manipulations
67. Persistence
68. Architecture
69. Method execution location
70. Multiple language interface
71. Object translation facilities
72. Backup and recovery facilities
73. Tools
74. 4GL
75. Change notification
76. Versioning
77. Configuration management
78. Standards
79. Rules
80. Platforms
81. Compilers
82. GUIs
83. Gateways
84. File systems

These evaluation criteria will be discussed in greater detail in the next chapter.

12.5 Nontechnical Issues

These can be broadly classified under the following categories:

Business criteria

Commitment to standards

Support capability

Customer references

These issues are discussed in detail later in this chapter.

12.6   Benchmarking an OODBMS

When new technology is employed, application software developers have to choose a product from an increasing number of vendors. The necessity of benchmarking cannot be overemphasized. Standard benchmarks may not be available for products that involve new technology. Those that are available may address synthetic examples and tend not to be comprehensive. This is the case with OODBMSs to date. The only viable option is to design and develop individual benchmarks for each software product. Lai and Guzenda have provided the following three steps in benchmarking planning:[1]

> *Establish clear goals:* It is very critical to establish clear goals at the beginning of the evaluation effort. Before you invest any time in designing a benchmark, you should first decide what you would like to measure. The primary purpose of a benchmark is to measure and compare the functionality and performance of different systems in such a way that the results can be meaningfully extrapolated to target applications. This requires identification of functional requirements and performance targets.
>
> *Communicate goals to vendors:* Vendor participation is important to the successful completion of the benchmarking effort. Vendors can bring in the experience of prior evaluations for other applications. Feedback from vendors will be very valuable. Vendors must be considered to be partners in the evaluation effort.
>
> *Establish firm project schedules:* Like any significant project, an evaluation effort needs to be estimated, scheduled, and managed. Evaluation efforts often have a tendency to expand and consume all available time and resources.

12.7   Evaluations: Benchmarking Applications to Test Throughput

The most important feature that should first be evaluated is the "throughput performance" characteristics. This involves identifying the throughput requirements of the application system and then evaluating the throughput delivered by the OODBMS. The following throughput-related issues must be addressed:

1. Object creation time

2. Object access time

3. Object update time

Some of these issues may be more important than others in user applications. The prototype application that is designed to evaluate the OODBMS must focus on those issues that are important.

In addition to object-related issues, throughput tests should also focus on the following:

1. Database creation times

2. Time to populate a database from scratch, up to the average size of the database

3. Time to create collections, containers, sets, arrays, and other structures that are used to group homogenous or heterogenous objects

Other performance-related issues that should be addressed are the following:

Physical device management

Clustered indexes and nonclustered indexes

Query optimization

12.8   Types of Data the Benchmark Should Test

Most applications contain some simple data types and a few complex data types. The data in some applications are more complex than those in others. In OODBMSs, the facility to store atomic data containing only scalar attributes is the minimum requirement. Groups of atomic objects, sometimes referred to as composite objects, are quite common in most applications. Composite objects are logical building blocks of the design. Larger objects can be created by assembling composite objects. The relationships between atomic objects and parts of composite objects may have to be modeled in some applications. The benchmark design should account for CRUD (Creation, Update, Deletion) operations on all these categories of objects.

12.9   Evaluations: Manipulations of Sets, Collections, etc.

In some applications, performing a task involves accessing all items in a container or set and updating some of them. This is usually done within a transaction using an iterative process. Such container, collection, or set manipulations require special prototypes that simulate the following:

1. Creation of sets, containers, collections, etc.

2. Accessing one item from a set or container or collection

3. Updating one item

4. Updating all items

5. Deleting one item

6. Deleting all items

12.10   Testing Typical Types of Transactions

Different applications have different types of transactions. The patterns of object access vary widely and are application-specific. The amount of work done in each transaction is not only application-specific but also programmer-dependent. A prototype used for performing benchmark tests must simulate the work done by typical transactions in the applications.

The time taken by a commit operation is an important issue in some applications. This is usually dependent upon the amount of work done in the transaction. It is also a function of the number of objects (items) accessed in the transaction.

12.11   Types of Queries That Need to Be Evaluated

The performance characteristics of the OODBMS are influenced by the types of queries used for the evaluations. There are several ways of performing a query and several ways of accessing an item in a database. OODBMS evaluations should focus on all of the following types of queries:

Associative queries of atomic parts

Associative queries of composite objects

Existential queries for atomic parts

Navigational queries

12.12   Scalability Issues

The problem with most product evaluation efforts is the scale of the prototype. If an OODBMS performs well under all test situations, it is likely to perform well in the actual application. However, if the complete application in its final form is a big and complex application with large amounts of data distributed over a network of servers, then issues of scale must be emphasized while testing each and every feature of the OODBMS.

Scalability can be addressed in many mutually orthogonal dimensions:

1. Scalability in terms of network size
2. Scalability in terms of actual amounts of data (objects)
3. Scalability in terms of computing power required
4. Scalability in terms of number of simultaneous instances of the final application that can concurrently be executed in the given environment

12.13 The Need to Test Interaction between OODBMS Features

Its not enough to evaluate all the features in an OODBMS. It also important to evaluate how the important features interact to provide various services. The number of possible feature interactions grows exponentially with the number of OODBMS features, and testing all such interactions is neither practical nor feasible. Jacob Stein has highlighted some of the important interactions between OODBMS features that must be part of the OODBMS evaluations:[2]

1. How do distribution and indexing interact: can the indexing mechanism index objects distributed across many places?
2. How do distribution and query evaluation interact: can objects that are distributed be accessed using a single query?
3. How do indexing and versioning interact: can versioned objects be indexed? If so, which version is indexed?
4. How do schema modification and versioning interact: can a single version history deal with an object whose class has been modified several times? Can classes themselves be versioned?
5. How does distribution interact with referential integrity: can the OODBMS prevent dangling references in a distributed environment? What happens when a reference from an object in one place to an object in another place is no longer valid?

12.14 Comparative Evaluations

Comparative evaluations of OODBMS (or any other systems) are a complicated effort. It is necessary to compare the different OODBMS simultaneously for meaningful results. It is generally not possible to perform a fair comparison if the competing systems being evaluated are not subjected to the same or similar tests and benchmarks. Each system must be used to the same degree, and each system must be tested with the same rigorous battery of tests.

Not all OODBMS will have all the same features. Some systems have more features than others. If a given feature is not provided by a vendor, its impact on the rest of the system and the application to be developed must be evaluated. The comparative evaluation should provide a good measure of which competing system is more functionally complete than the others.

It is also important to verify that the claims made by the vendors are true. Oftentimes, vendors make claims that are only partially supported. A proper evaluation will result in highlighting those areas that need further clarification from vendors.

12.15 An Exercise in Modeling the Throughput Analysis

To help in the evaluations, it is important to create mathematical models of the application and verify the throughput requirements. In this section, we will describe a typical scenario where OODBMS are used, and model the throughput by mathematical equations.

The environment

The hardware configuration for this exercise is a network of 10 servers. The applications are mostly interactive services that may be executed over a network of 100 workstations that have access to the data on the 10 servers. In addition, noninteractive services can be executed on the servers. We will assume that each workstation has 2 services executing simultaneously and that the server has 30 services running concurrently. A typical database application can be expected to use 7 services on the average.

The model of the applications/services

Services can be broadly separated into two types:

T_1 Noninteractive services
T_2 Interactive services

The T_1 type of services can be further classified as:

Simple Manipulation (SM) services, which take single-digit time (in millisecs, t_{sm} = rand % 10) to process, and

Massive Queries (MQ), which can take several seconds to finish (t_{mq} = rand % 10 secs).

T_2 type services can typically take (t_{inter}, in the range of) single-digit minutes to complete.

If there are n functionally different types of services available, assuming for the sake of this exercise that they are all equally likely to be invoked,

$t_1 = \text{sizeof}(T_1)$ the size of function returns the size or cardinality.

$t_2 = \text{sizeof}(T_2)$

$n = t_1 + t_2$

$\text{smsz} = \text{sizeof}(SM)$

$\text{mqsz} = \text{sizeof}(MQ)$

$t_1 = \text{smsz} + \text{mqsz}$

Total number of interactive services on the network at any given time
= number of services per workstation · number of workstations

$= 2 \cdot 100 = 200$ services

Total number of batch/noninteractive services on the network at any given time = number of services per server · number of servers

$= 30 \cdot 10 = 300$ services

Assuming that the services are equally likely, at any given instant of time there will be $300/t_1$ instances of each T_1 type of services, and $200/t_2$ instances of each T_2 type service.

The number of user applications per second serviced by each of the SM services = $1/t_{sm}$.

The number of service requests, per second, satisfied by each MQ type service = $1/t_{mq}$.

The number of service requests satisfied, per second, by each of the T_2 type interactive services = $1/t_{inter}$.

The total number of service requests satisfied by all the services in 1 s is

$$(300/t_1) \cdot \text{smsz}/t_{sm} + (300/t_1) \cdot \text{mqsz}/t_{mq} + 200/t_{inter}$$

Let us assume that the number of new user applications appear at the rate of `appl_rate` per second.

Let us also assume that each user application requires `num_ser` number of services. Then,

Total number of services requested = num_serv · appl_rate

Assuming a state of equilibrium,

The total number of service requests satisfied by all the services in 1 s = the total number of services requested by the `appl_rate` number of applications

Therefore,

$$(300/t_1) \cdot \mathrm{smsz}/t_{sm} + (300/t_1) \cdot \mathrm{mqsz}/t_{mq} + 200/t_{inter} = \text{num\_serv} \cdot \text{appl\_rate}$$

$$(300/t_1)(\mathrm{smsz}/t_{sm} + \mathrm{mqsz}/t_{mq}) + 200/t_{inter} = \text{num\_serv} \cdot \text{appl\_rate}$$

If we parameterize the number of workstations (num-work) and servers (num-servers), we get

$$(30 \cdot \text{num-servers})/t_1(\mathrm{smsz}/t_{sm} + \mathrm{mqsz}/t_{mq}) + \text{num-work} \cdot 2/t_{inter}$$
$$= \text{numserv} \cdot \text{appl\_rate}$$

To simplify these equations, let us make the following assumptions:

An SM type service employs a transaction that makes 4 database accesses plus one update.

An MQ type service employs a transaction that makes a 1000 SM type data access (presumably in a loop of 1000) plus one update.

Again assume 0.08 s per warm database access, and 0.7 s for an update including the commit.

Assuming $t_1 = 20$, with smsz = mqsz = 10, we get

$$t_{sm} = 4 \cdot 0.08 + 0.7$$

$$t_{mq} = 1000(4 \cdot 0.08) + 0.7$$

If the interactive services take $t_{inter} = 600$ s to execute, the number of services that each user application makes use of is num_serv = 7, the number of servers in the system is num_servers = 10, and the number of workstations in the system is num_work = 100, then we get

$$\text{appl\_rate} = 22$$

This implies that such a system can handle approximately 22 user applications per second. If we consider each user application to be a transaction, then such an environment would support 22 transactions per second (TPS).

12.16   Business Criteria

Often, the best technology might come embodied in a product developed by a company that is neither financially stable nor technically mainstream. Therefore, it not wise to ignore business reasons while performing product evaluations. In general, vendors must meet the following criteria before their product can be purchased:

1. The vendor company must be financially stable and healthy.
2. The vendor must be in a situation to harness new technology.
3. The vendor should be able to provide periodic upgrades to the product.
4. The vendor must have strategic alliances with leaders in related technologies.
5. The vendor should not be opposed by an overwhelming alliance of other vendors in the industry.
6. The technology offered by the vendor must have a high probability of surviving rival technologies.

12.17   Commitment to Standards

Most applications today are being run in heterogenous environments in the presence of a variety of technologies. With several competing technologies to choose from to address any given project requirement, there is likely to be a high rate of obsolescence in the industry. Because of the intense competition among vendors, there is a need to avoid wasteful product developments. This is being achieved by the establishment of standards for any given technology.

An OODBMS is likely to be only one component, albeit an important one, among several components of an application in the user's work environment. Because of the diversity of applications and tools available in engineering environments, an OODBMS must provide *connectivity* between tools and environments, and broad *interoperability* of applications. Interoperability and connectivity are possible only if the vendor of the OODBMS adheres to industry standards and participates in creating new standards.

Standards for OO technology in general, and OODBMS in particular, are likely to emerge in the next 5 years. Several industry groups have formed consortiums to address specific problem areas in the current technology. Several OODBMS vendors have pledged support for the various industry and research groups trying to establish standards.

12.18 Customer Support Capability

It is not enough to buy a good product from a vendor. It is important to have good and timely product support from the vendor. Customer support reflects the vendor's overall commitment to quality. It also reflects the financial state of a company. Without an adequate number of customer support personnel, a vendor may not be able to meet the technical support requirements of the customer base.

12.19 Customer References

Good recommendations from other satisfied customers are often a good indication of quality service and quality products. Vendors are often eager to provide references of satisfied clients. However, it is important to identify the differences between the current project requirements and the project requirements of the references provided by the vendor. It is a good idea to contact as many satisfied customers of the vendor as possible before making a big investment in the vendor's products.

12.20 OODBMS Evaluation: Example Code

A program designed to test the totally random access of elements of a document in a document store database is presented in this section. Using the document store example, the program tries to find the OODBMS performance by accessing databases and containers at random to update elements in document objects. This can be considered a test to evaluate the average time taken for typical database updates.

The outline of this evaluation test is as follows:

1. Given the total number of databases, the number of documents in each database, and the typical number of segments or elements in a typical document, the test tries to identify the average time taken to update an randomly accessed element. The database, document, and element are all randomly selected.

2. The test is repeated several times in a loop to get a good average.

3. The Federated Database is opened only once.

4. The transaction is committed only once, after all the items have been updated.

There can be several other possible variations to this test. Such tests must reflect the actual access patterns in the actual application environment for the average update times to be meaningful.

```
/*
 *        eval_loop_upd.C: In a loop, access databases and
 *                         containers at random to update.
 *                         The commit is outside the loop.
 */

#include <oo.h> // Objectivity/DB system header file
#include <ooSchema.h> // Objectivity/DB system header file
#include "doc.h" // User DDL schema header file
#include <string.h>
#include <stream.h>
#include <iostream.h>
#include <stdio.h>
#include <stdlib.h>

main( int argc, char** argv)
{
    char oidvar[30];
    filebuf outbuf;
    ostream outfile(&outbuf);

    if (argc < 5)
    {
        fprintf(stderr, "Usage: %s num_loop tot_docs tot_docs tot_segs
outfile\n",
        argv[0]);
        exit(1);
    }

    char trail[50], timestr[20];
    int num_loop = atoi(argv[1]);
    int tot_docs = atoi(argv[2]);
    int tot_docs = atoi(argv[3]);
    int tot_segs = atoi(argv[4]);
    strcpy(trail, argv[5]);

/////////////////////////////////////////////////////////////
//
// Initialize Objectivity/DB
//
/////////////////////////////////////////////////////////////

    ooInit(12, 200, 1000);

    /* Start Transaction */
    ooTrans transaction;
    transaction.start();

    // Open the Federated Database

    ooHandle(ooFDObj) federatedDBH;
    if (federatedDBH.open("eval_objy", oocUpdate) != oocSuccess) {
        fprintf(stderr, "ERROR: Cannot open eval_objy Federated
Database.\n");
        transaction.abort();
        exit(1);
    }
```

```
if (outbuf.open(trail, output) = = 0)
{
  cerr << "Cannot open output file \n";
  exit (1);
}

for (int i = 0; i < num_loop; i++)
{
  const char *source = "DOC_SRC_";
  char doc_source[60], intstr[20];
  if (i = = 400)
      ooRunStatus();

    strcpy(doc_source, source);
    int doc_num;
    while ((doc_num = (rand()% tot_docs)) = = 0){}
    sprintf(intstr, "%d", doc_num);
    strcat(doc_source, intstr);
    puts(doc_source);
  outfile << "Starting access of Document source:"
    << doc_source << ":"
    << time(0) << "\n";
  outfile.flush();
//////////////////////////////////////////////////////////
//
// Open the Database
//////////////////////////////////////////////////////////
      ooHandle(ooDBObj) databasedoc;
                  // Open for Update
      if(databasedoc.open(federatedDBH, doc_source, oocUpdate)
        != oocSuccess)
  {
      fprintf(stderr, "ERROR: Cannot open docsource Database.\n");
      transaction.abort();
      exit(1);
  }
        /* access the document in database */
      strcpy(oidvar, "oid");
      int doc_num = rand()%tot_docs;
      sprintf(intstr, "%d", doc_num);
      strcat(oidvar, intstr);
      puts(oidvar);
      // access the ise in the default container of
      // the databasedoc database object.
      ooHandle(ise) ise_h;
      if (ise_h.lookupObj(databasedoc, oidvar) != oocSuccess)
  {
      fprintf(stderr,
        "ERROR: ise '%s' does not exist .\n", oidvar);
      transaction.abort();
      exit(1);
  }

    outfile << "accessing database for ise:"
      << oidvar << " : "
      << time(0) << "\n";
    outfile.flush();

    ooHandle(ooContObj) cont_H;
    cont_H = (ise_h->bodyH())->cont_R;
    if( cont_H.open() != oocSuccess)
  {
```

```
      fprintf(stderr,
    ,   "ERROR: ise '%s' does not exist .\n", oidvar);
      transaction.abort();
      exit(1);
}

   char segvar[20];
strcpy(segvar, "segid");
   int seg = rand()%tot_segs;
   sprintf(intstr, "%d", seg);
   strcat(segvar, intstr);
   puts(segvar);

   outfile << "accessing database for element:"
           << segvar << " : "
           << time(0) << "\n";

ooHandle(element) el_H;
   if(el_H.lookupObj(cont_H, segvar) != oocSuccess)
{
      fprintf(stderr,
        "ERROR: ise '%s' does not exist .\n", oidvar);
      transaction.abort();
      exit(1);
}

   ooVString elstr = "changing string-xxxxxxxxx-";
   el_H->setelement(elstr); // UPDATE
   puts(elstr);
   outfile << "element accessed:"
           << segvar << " : "
           << time(0) << "\n";
}

ooRunStatus();

outfile << "End of access of element in Document sources:"
        << time(0) << "\n";
outfile.flush();

////////////////////////////////////////////////////////////
//
// Shutdown Objectivity/DB
//
////////////////////////////////////////////////////////////

federatedDBH.close(); // Close the Federated Database
transaction.commit(); // Commit the transaction

exit(0); // Exit
}
```

References

1. Larry K. W. Lai and Leon Guzenda, "How to Benchmark an OODBMS," *Journal of Object-Oriented Programming,* 1991.
2. Jacob Stein, "Evaluating Object Database Management Systems," *Journal of Object-Oriented Programming,* vol. 5, no. 6, 1992, pp. 71–74.
3. Tim Connors and Peter Lyngback, "Providing Uniform Access to Heterogenous Information Bases," *Lecture Notes in Computer Science, Advances in Object-Oriented Database Systems, 2nd International Workshop on Object-Oriented Database Systems,* Springer-Verlag, 1988.

13

Evaluation of OODBMS:
The Important Criteria

Introduction

This chapter is dedicated to exploring the issues related to the evaluation of object-oriented databases. The criteria for selecting an OODBMS for an application domain should be specified with a lot of care and foresight. The features that are more important than others must be emphasized and thoroughly tested during the evaluation.

13.1 Persistence

Persistence can be visualized in two ways:[1]

1. Values are persistent, implying that they retain their identity and their persistence independent of who points to them.
2. Variables are persistent, which implies that persistence is retained only for values pointed to by persistent variables and, perhaps, that identity is associated more with the source of the pointer than with the destination of the pointer.

In C++, this distinction is obvious to the programmer, and different C++ OODBs tend to go in one direction or the other.

Researchers have identified four different models for indicating persistence:[1]

1. Universal persistence: persistent memory where everything is persistent.

2. Persistence by creation (allocation time): Instances of a class can be declared as either persistent or temporary. This implies the existence of *new* and *persistent new* operations. Persistence is orthogonal to type.

3. Persistence by type (inheritance): persistence objects are instances of a class which inherits a persistent mixin. All instances of a type are persistent; transient instances are of a different class and type. In such environments, persistence is associated with certain base classes and all classes derived from those persistent base classes.

4. Persistence at arbitrary times: this model subsumes the three described above and adds the ability to declare an object of arbitrary type to be persistent at some time after it is allocated. This is usually done by invoking a *persist* method on an object.

When preexisting class libraries are used, one problem usually encountered is that of identifying which user-defined objects are going to be persistent and which are going to be transient. When persistent objects, especially those provided by class libraries, make references to transient objects, there may be problems. That is because when the program ends, the transient objects disappear and the persistent objects are left with dangling references.

The key motivation for OODBMS is persistence of objects (Fig. 13.1). Prior to the OODBMS, only data could be persistent in databases,

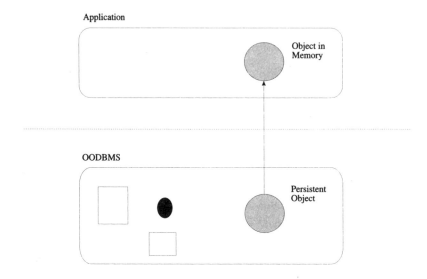

Figure 13.1 Persistence of objects.

necessitating the conversion of objects into pure data structures to obtain persistence. The OODBMS thus provides a better model of persistence.

Persistence in an OODBMS must be as unobtrusive as possible to the application developers; i.e., object persistence should require as little additional coding by the application developers as possible.

13.2 Architecture

An object-oriented database architecture adapts and scales more easily than relational databases to handle any amount of data. The ability to migrate objects from database to database is another advantage of an OODBMS. OODBMS architecture must support the transparent distribution of data from database applications. It is possible to design a specific part of an OO application to deal with distribution while the bulk of the application and class libraries are designed to be independent of the location of the objects.

13.3 Atomicity of Transactions

Atomicity deals with the transaction system's ability to commit or roll back proposed changes to the state of the computational system. A transaction is to be considered as a unit of operation. The semantics of transactions are not the same in all OODBMSs. In general, a transaction implies that either all the operations within the transactions are successfully completed or none of them are completed. This is sometimes referred to as "all or nothing" semantics. The transaction management subsystem must provide an atomic commit capability for sets of storage objects. It should also enforce concurrency control by locking objects or collections of objects.

Transactions are expected to help maintain atomicity in the presence of all the following error conditions:

Deadlocks

Database system software failures

Application software failures

CPU failures

Disk crashes

13.4 Consistency of Transactions

A transaction is expected to change the database from one consistent state to another. As such, different transactions should not affect one another. In particular, a transaction should not overwrite precommitted data of another transaction. A transaction should also not commit any writes until the transaction is completed. Again, a transaction should not read precommitted data from other transactions. In general, the changes due to a transaction should not be visible to other transactions until the transaction completes and commits successfully.

An OODB transaction has been viewed by some researchers from the point of making forward progress. The purpose of transactions is to ensure forward progress through a sequence of intermediate consistent states. An OODB transaction must map persistent and transient data from one consistent state to a new consistent state. A system can enforce consistency either explicitly by evaluating a set of predicates or implicitly by assuming that each transaction preserves consistency when running without interference from others.[3]

13.5   Isolation of Internal State of a Transaction

While a transaction is being executed, its internal state is not visible to other transactions. A transaction should not reveal its results to other concurrent transactions until it commits. If a transaction aborts, it should leave the database in a consistent state. In some OODBMSs, it is not possible to use in one transaction a pointer which was assigned in another transaction. When a transaction is being executed, all objects that are accessed by the transaction for writing or updating will typically be locked from concurrent access by other transactions. In some OODBMSs, if links to remote machines are established within a transaction, or some other nondatabase activity is initiated, a transaction failure may not be able to roll back the nondatabase-related side effects of the transaction.

13.6   Durability of the Results of a Transaction

Durability means that none of the updates made by a transaction should be lost once the transaction is completed successfully and has been committed. This is also referred to as persistence of the results of transactions. Durability is related to hardware reliability and strategies to compensate for hardware failures, especially problems with RAM and disk storage.

It is very important to verify that the results of a transaction are as they should be. The transaction should leave the database in a consistent state. The database should be rolled back to a consistent state after a database failure. It should also be rolled back to a consistent state after an application software failure, after a CPU failure, and after a disk failure.

13.7   Long Transactions

OODBMSs should support both regular transactions and long transactions. Long transactions can last for hours. Some of them can last weeks or months. If long transactions are supported by the OODBMS, the checkpointing facility should also be provided.

Persistent long transactions are an extreme case of long transactions, where the long transaction can span system shutdown or failures.

13.8   Nested Transactions

A nested transaction is a way of grouping operations as an atomic step within a transaction.

Some OODBMSs support nested transactions. For example, ObjectStore provides for transactions within transactions. The semantics of nested transactions can vary across OODBMSs. In general, if the outer transaction fails, the inner transactions must be rolled back.

13.9   Shared Transactions

It may be possible to allow multiple processes or users to participate in the same transaction. This feature is not generally supported by OODBMSs. Some OODBMSs permit sets of actors to cooperate explicitly to solve problems in a coordinated manner. This requires the relaxation of the isolation constraint in transactions.

13.10   Nonblocking Read Consistency

Some OODBMSs support nonblocking read consistency. This is possible only if the objects being shared among concurrent transactions can be locked for multiple-read. Some OODBMSs permit multiple-read–one-write (MROW) facilities.

13.11   Concurrency Control Issues

Concurrency control strategies can be broadly categorized into the following categories:

Optimistic: assumes that simultaneous access to the same objects is rare and conflict is checked at commit time. Conflicts at commit time result in transaction abort or restart.

Pessimistic: Checks) for access conflicts at the time the lock is requested, with some locks queued until the conflict is resolved. No conflicts are present at commit time.

Within the framework of a transaction/commit protocol, some OODBMS developers have elected to control concurrent access to shared objects via a variant of two-phase locking. This is in contrast to an optimistic concurrency control mechanism, in which serializability is realized by aborting transactions that conflict. During a transaction, a session must obtain a shared object before it can be accessed. Thus commit operations do not fail. Unfortunately, the transactions in such a scheme can block waiting to acquire a shared object. A test-and-lock mechanism needs to be provided to test whether an object can be obtained without blocking. In a previous chapter, other concurrency control mechanisms were also dealt with.

The pessimistic mode of concurrency control is most suitable for environments where there tends to be a high probability of data conflicts among transactions. The optimistic mode of concurrency control is appropriate for applications with little or no data conflict among transactions.

13.12   Lock Promotion and Lock Escalation

In some OODBMSs, when an object is first accessed, it is locked using read locks. A read lock can be upgraded to a write lock when an object is first updated. If objects are accessed using write locks, the lock cannot be changed to a read lock. Objects that are cached in memory outside a transaction boundary are subjected to null locks and notify locks. Null locks and notify locks can be exchanged with each other in most OODBMSs. Such objects must be refetched with either a read or a write lock when the object is needed inside a transaction.

In some OODBMSs, when a composite object is first accessed, all the objects to which the composite object is linked are locked. In others, only the parent object is locked when first accessed, and subcomponents are locked as they are subsequently accessed. It is good to have automatic escalation of the granularity of locking to a higher level of granularity.

13.13   Locks Set and Release

In some OODBMSs, the objects are locked automatically when an object is first accessed, and the lock is released automatically when the transaction terminates. In others, objects have to be explicitly locked and released before they can be accessed. In such OODBMSs, applications have the responsibility to set locks and release them subsequently.

13.14 Granularity of Locks

Probably the most important issue of concurrency is the granularity of locking provided by the OODBMS. Nondatabase applications generally provide file-level locking. In an OODBMS, the two common modes of locking are page-level locking and object-level locking. In general, the granularity of locked data can be

- dirage
- An object
- A cluster of objects
- An object graph
- A partition of a database
- A database
- A collection of databases

Page-level locking can be acceptable for applications that will be used by only a small number of concurrent users. To achieve greater concurrency, the objects that are usually used together can be grouped and placed together on the same page. Object-level locking should enable more concurrency.

Strickland has this to say about locking:[3]

> Most of the object databases provide a locking model that I will call the *standard read/write locking model*. This locking model guarantees you several nice characteristics, including serializability, noninterference with other transactions, the ability to abort transactions, and protection against deadlocks. But the amount of concurrency you can achieve with this model is inherently limited, largely because a write lock is not compatible with any other read or write lock. Contention for locks usually appears first at fairly predictable places, such as root objects, at class objects, or within database indices.

13.15 Deadlock Detection

Deadlock can occur among transactions in any database that employs a pessimistic mode of concurrency control. The following are some of the techniques for solving them:

- Deadlock prevention

- Deadlock avoidance
- Deadlock detection
- Deadlock resolution

The choice of any of these techniques is application-dependent. Some applications may not tolerate deadlock detection. For example, a CIM application that controls a robotic arm on a factory floor cannot have a transaction aborted because of deadlock.

13.16 Backup and Recovery Facilities

Recovery can be broadly categorized into three types:

- Abort recovery
- Crash recovery
- Recovery from media failure

In conventional approaches, recovery and durability are treated together because what is done to make updates durable is at the same time the problem for atomicity when an abort occurs.

13.17 Object Translation Facilities

The object translation mechanism is responsible for mapping storage objects among the representations that they assume in computational memory, in long-term storage, and when being passed from machine to machine. Object translation involves determining the boundaries of storage objects and identifying what is encapsulated within the object.

In systems that support object translation, when an object is saved into persistent storage, the object translation mechanism is invoked to translate the various storage objects encountered, beginning with the storage object at the root of the specific persistent object.

13.18 Standards

An OODBMS must provide broad connectivity between tools and environments. Interoperability of applications should be supported. This is possible only if the OODBMS is designed to adhere to industry standards, and if the vendor is committed to incorporating newer standards as they are developed. The important industry standard efforts relevant to OODBMSs are

- Object Management Group (OMG)

- X/Open Distributed Transaction Processing
- ANSI C++
- X3/SPARC/DBSSG/OODB Task Group, and its successor
- X3H7 Object Information Management (OIM)
- OSI Transaction Processing Standard
- Open Systems Foundation (OSF)

The OMG is a consortia of over 100 OOT vendors building an OO *application integration framework*. It has several subgroups, three of which are relevant to this topic: OMG OM Task Force, OMG OODB SIG, and the OMG ORB Task Force. The OMG OM Task Force is a subgroup in OMG responsible for defining and adopting technology leading to an interoperable Object Model. The OMG OODB SIG is responsible for writing a white paper on how OODBs fit the OMG architecture. The OMG ORB Task Force is responsible for adopting a commercial object communications layer for use within the OMG. Such a communications layer would be based on the message-passing paradigm, designed as a bus called the Object Request Broker (ORB).

The X3/SPARC/DBSSG/OODB Task Group was the object-oriented database task group (OODBTG) of the Database Systems Study Group (DBSSG), which is one of the advisory groups to the Accredited Standards Committee X3 (ASC/X3), Standards Planning and Requirements Committee (SPARC), operating under the procedures of ANSI.

13.19 Multiple Language Interface

Most OODBMSs have selected a particular programming language and implemented persistent storage for the language. This has resulted in a tight coupling between the storage mechanisms and the constructs available in the programming language. There is a pressing need to be able to support multiple language interfaces for the same storage mechanisms. Some researchers have proposed that multiple language support is best provided by a common, low-level kernel that would provide functionality that can be used at higher levels to implement various language servers.

13.20 Location Independence in Distributed Database System

In a distributed database system, if applications have to be truly portable and flexible, the OODB system must provide location independence. The actual location of the objects must be known only to the OODB while the applications are provided access to any object that is persistent in the OODB.

It is difficult to determine the exact needs with regards to distribution, but it is of utmost importance. Very few applications make effective use of the distribution facilities of databases. Stein makes this observation:[4] "The only way to know how well a product supports distribution is to test it yourself or speak to someone who has. The database industry is littered with fancy distribution architectures that many years after the initial deployment have not as yet delivered on their apparent promise."

13.21   Local Autonomy at Each Site

In distributed database systems, the various applications have to cooperate in successfully completing their computing tasks. While the user applications have their control from a server or a workstation, the databases that are distributed over a network can have a centralized model of cooperation or an autonomous model of cooperation. Traditionally, implementing a centralized model of control and cooperation has been easier than implementing a decentralized and autonomous (distributed) model of cooperation. In a distributed system, at the minimum, it should be possible to grant local autonomy for the following activities:

1. Local database management
2. Local locking
3. Local recovery
4. Local transaction management
5. Local communications management

Some OODBMSs that apparently support distributed computing employ a centralized lock manager that tends to become a bottleneck.

13.22   Fragmentation and Replication Independence

Some OODBMSs support fragmented objects. The fragmented object can be viewed as a set of elementary objects instantiated in different address spaces cooperating closely with one another, making sure that other objects do not interfere with the overall structure and functionality of the fragmented object. To the clients of such objects, the fragmented object appears as a single one, and the location of the individual component objects constituting the fragmented object should be transparent to the users. Such location transparency is only for the clients of the object; implementors of the object will usually be aware of the distribution.

Replication is used to improve the overall system efficiency in the following three ways:

1. Improving availability of objects in the presence of concurrency control and fragile distribution

2. Improving locality in the presence of distribution

3. Improving computational speed by keeping replicas in different formats, generally in the presence of heterogeneity

13.23   Distributed Transaction Processing

The advantage of distributed OODBMSs is that they offer complete support for transaction processing. It is difficult to guarantee consistency among heterogenous databases if distributed updates are supported. A distributed transaction accesses objects from multiple sites. Without special coordination among individual transaction managers, it is impossible.

One approach to distributed transactions is to create one local transaction for each participating site, on behalf of the distributed transaction, to move data in and out of the local database at each site. At commit, all the local transactions must coordinate among themselves through a two-phase commit protocol.

13.24   Distributed Query Processing

In a distributed database system, there is a tradeoff between[5]

1. Running a query on a remote database and transmitting the results back to the importing database

2. Transmitting data from a remote database to the importing database for local processing

13.25   Hardware Independence

Most OODBMSs have been ported to most of the popular hardware platforms. Support for client/server architecture also indicates a commitment to hardware independence. Some OODBMSs may be limited to certain hardware platforms because of their reliance on specific operating systems. It is important to evaluate the ability and commitment of a vendor to keep up with the emerging hardware platforms and related technologies.

13.26 Operating System and Network Independence

It is important to select an OODBMS that is available on the largest number of operating systems, with support for the greatest number of networks. OODBMSs that employ operating systems and networks that are popular and widely used are a better choice than those that do not. It is also important to evaluate the ability and commitment of a vendor to keep up with changes in operating systems and related software.

13.27 Object Model

The choice of an object model for the OODBMS determines the model of transactions, the query language, and several other features of the OODBMS. In general, the object model should provide for the specification of static properties of a database, namely, the entities, entity attributes, and entity relationships; the dynamic properties of databases namely, entity operations, attribute operations, and relationship operations; and integrity constraints for permissible database states and permissible state transitions.

13.28 Dynamic Binding and Polymorphism

The availability of polymorphism and dynamic binding facilities is more a function of the programming language interface to the OODBMS than of the inherent design of the OODBMS itself. Some OODBMSs provide a C interface that does not provide any support for polymorphism or dynamic binding. This is generally due to the inability of the programming language interface to incorporate the concepts. Using C++ interface libraries, both polymorphism and dynamic binding can be achieved in most OODBMSs.

13.29 Encapsulation

In an OODBMS, encapsulation refers to the ability to store code with data in the database. In most OODBMSs, it is possible to obtain a clean separation between the external interface of an object and its internal implementation because of the encapsulation and information hiding facilities.

13.30   Object Identity

The strength of the object identity supported by different OODBMSs can be very different. The strength of the object identity can be measured in terms of robustness, expressiveness, and redundancy. Addressing this issue, Strickland[3] states,

> Different object databases offer different kinds of identity. An object database might have an option to name objects only by an address in a memory space. This feature is designed for simplicity, performance, and low memory overhead when all goes right, but beware the risks that come with it if anything goes wrong. Another naming option is to have an arbitrary "logical object identifier" for each object, where the identifiers are in the order of 64 to 128 bits, and are guaranteed never to be reused. This is a big improvement, as it guards against the problem of writing into the middle of some other object because the object you wanted to use was deleted. It also gives you the flexibility to migrate objects because you are not naming them by their physical location. But arbitrary identifiers lack the robustness of character string file names, and meaningful object names are a better approach.

13.31   Types and Classes

Some OODBMSs treat classes as first class objects. This provides great flexibility. Such systems are usually based on Smalltalk or CLOS. Very few systems based on C++ have this feature.

Objects can be grouped into types by commonality of behavior or by commonality of implementation.

13.32   Inheritance and Delegation

Most class-based systems provide support for inheritance as a mechanism for sharing behavior and attributes. Delegation as a mechanism for code sharing is not very common among OODBMS products. Most OODBMSs provide a C++ interface to the database, and C++ employs inheritance for sharing behavior and attributes rather than delegation. As such, delegation is quite often not supported.

13.33   Relationship and Attributes

Most OODBMSs provide support for the following kinds of relationships:

1:1

1:n

$n{:}1$

$n{:}m$

In general, relationships are named bidirectional links between related objects. Relationships can be treated as objects in some OODBMSs. In such systems, relationships can have attributes themselves.

13.34   Literal Data Types

While some OODBMSs treat everything as an object, most don't go that far. Quite often, simple entities such as numbers and character strings are treated as literals. Some OODBMSs also provide support for literals like date, time, and money.

13.35   Multimedia Objects

Conventional databases could not effectively support multimedia data. OODBMSs, in general, provide strong support for complex data such as multimedia. Most OODBMSs provide the facilities to store and retrieve video and audio data. However, nontraditional data such as images and audio segments require a great amount of disk memory to save. Moreover, being able to name and subsequently query such data requires the use of non-value-based querying techniques.

13.36   Aggregate Objects

It is very important to have class libraries that can help create aggregate objects such as collections, sets, bags, lists, B-trees, etc. OODB applications often make heavy use of such aggregate objects. In some OODBMSs, all objects by default belong to a collection or a container.

13.37   Composite and Complex Objects

Several application domains require the ability to define and manipulate a set of objects as a single logical entity. Some of the reasons for this are

1. Semantic integrity
2. Efficient storage and retrieval

Composite objects are used to specify a hierarchy of exclusive component objects. The hierarchy of classes to which the objects belong is referred to as the *composite object hierarchy*. Some researchers consider a composite object to be that part of a conventional nested object concept on which the IS-PART-OF relationship has been imposed.

Composite objects augment the semantic integrity of an object-oriented data model through the notion of *dependent objects*. A dependent object is defined as an object that is contained within another object, being owned by exactly one object. Thus, its existence depends on the existence of another object, termed the *root* object.

A composite object may be used as a unit for clustering related objects in the OODBMS. When the root object is accessed by an application, all or most of the dependent objects are also likely to be accessed. Thus, it is efficient to store all constituents of a composite object as close to one another as possible on secondary storage.

13.38   Integrity

Integrity is very important in databases because an error state or a bug introduced in the persistent data has the potential to cause problems in the database which can affect all future users of that database. An OODBMS can automatically perform integrity checking when a change occurs to a persistent object because the change takes place in the database. In complex objects, referential integrity can be handled easily by the use of bidirectional associations or links.

13.39   Schema Extensibility

The ability to change the definition of classes and provide mechanisms for accessing existing instances of changed classes is termed *schema extensibility* or *schema evolution*. Most OODBMSs provide some support for schema evolution. They differ mostly in their strategies for migrating existing objects (instances of changed classes) to conform to newer class definitions. In some OODBMSs, simple changes to class definitions do not require any evolution and can be handled automatically by the OODBMS. For example, adding a new class or changing method access from private to public (or vice versa) does not necessitate schema evolution in most OODBMSs. In some OODBMSs, adding or deleting any of the following does not necessitate evolution:

1. Indexes
2. Virtual member functions
3. Non-virtual member functions
4. Static data members

Schema evolution is generally required when the memory layout is modified by changes to the definition of the classes. In some cases, evolution can be handled automatically by the OODBMS. In other situations, the changes to application schema can be so drastic as to require the specification of exception handlers or transformer functions.

13.40 Version Control

Different OODBMSs differ in the following issues related to versioning:

- Creation of new versions
- Referencing versions other than the current versions
- Existence of any versioning mechanisms and, if they exist, whether they support linear versioning, branch versioning, or both
- Mechanisms for merging branched versions
- Protocols for referencing a versioned object
- Separate identity for each version of an object

Some OODBMSs employ explicit version creation and symbolic names for version control, while others employ timestamps as identifying keys to locate a given version. The timestamp-based version control has several advantages—it is easier to identify a configuration that existed at a certain time, rather than having to find all the version numbers that make up a given configuration.

Some OODBMSs support linear versioning, others support branch versioning, and a few support both versioning schemes. Linear versioning can lead to simplified logging schemes. Transactions accessing data of different branches of versions do not interfere with each other.

13.41 Configuration Management

Both concrete prespecified configurations and dynamic configurations should ideally be supported by the OODBMS. Generic configuration management allows a version of a parent object to bind to a generic child version that may have been created later than the parent. Thus, the creation of a new version of an object does not trigger the creation of parent objects in the structured hierarchy of objects.

An important issue encountered in configuration management systems is expressed by the following question: Do objects "know" that they are part of a configuration of objects? Some OODBMSs allow the objects to keep track of configurations that they are part of.

13.42 Query Language

Some OODBMSs employ the host language as the query language. Others provide an extension to the host language as a query language. A major use of a query language is the retrieval and update of instances of collection types based on predicates formulated on the structural and behavioral properties of objects.

In some OODBMSs, SQL is used as an ad hoc query language. Most object query languages provide declarative access to objects stored in collections. OO systems tend to employ navigation rather than SQL type selection in order to find objects.

13.43   Query Optimization

Query optimization results in the transformation of queries expressed in terms of high-level language statements into equivalent query execution plans that carry out the execution of queries efficiently. The query optimizer should be extensible. In relational databases, query optimization depends upon the algebraic properties of the relational operations, as well as the physical structure of relations. Query optimization in relational databases is made easy by the existence of a standard set of operations across all data. This is not the case with an OODBMS, since operations are defined on a per-type basis. In traditional query optimizers, the optimizer makes use of a scheduler and a cost estimation component. The scheduler makes use of the information provided by the cost estimation component. In an OODBMS, the cost estimation information can be encapsulated within each object, and cost estimation can be made a function of the objects themselves. Thus method computation costs can be computed by the objects themselves. Query optimization thus becomes distributed.

13.44   Indexing

An index represents a relationship among several database objects, namely, index objects, indexed objects, and collections. It must be possible to ensure the consistency of the indices in the presence of object updates. The problem of index maintenance is related to two other issues:[6]

1. Determining when to update and index
2. Determining how to update it

Indices can be updated immediately when an object participating in an index is updated, at transaction commit time, on demand just before the next time the index is used to compute a query, or by invalidating the index and rebuilding it.

13.45   Queries in Programs

If the object model used in the design of the OODB is programming language neutral (PLN), the level of sharing of data across applications developed in different programming languages will be increased. This is usually achieved by extending relational or semantic data models with object-oriented features.

In the programming-language-specific (PLS) approach to OODB design, the object data model is equivalent to the type system of an existing programming language. This can ameliorate the impedance mismatch problem. Several commercial OODBMSs have taken this approach, usually employing C/C++ as the object data model. ObjectStore, Versant, Ontos, and E are all based on C/C++.

13.46 Query Language Completeness

When a new type of object is added to the system, it must be queriable. Query languages for objects should provide support for the following:

1. Object identities and their manipulation
2. Encapsulation and data abstraction
3. Type inheritance
4. Complex objects
5. Polymorphism
6. User-defined collections
7. Heterogenous collections
8. Subsumes the relational algebra, or is at least as powerful as the relational algebra
9. Path expressions
10. Identity manipulation operators
11. Set comparison operators
12. Function invocations

A query language where the results of queries in the language have the same structural and behavioral properties as the objects on which the queries operate is said to have the *closure* property. This property is important in a query language because:[6]

1. It allows queries to be applied on results of previous queries.
2. It allows arbitrary composition of queries, which increases the opportunities for optimization.
3. It allows queries to be stored as derived objects in the database.

Object query languages should be closed over the collection types on which queries are allowed.

References

1. David Wells, "DARPA Open Object-Oriented Database Preliminary Module Specification: Persistence Policy Manager," Texas Instruments Inc., Version 2, Nov. 24, 1991.
2. Chung C. Wang, "DARPA Open Object-Oriented Database Preliminary Module Specification: Extended Transactions," Texas Instruments Inc., Version 2, Nov. 25, 1991.
3. Henry Strickland, "Three Giant Leaps for C++ Objects," *C++ Report*, vol. 4, no. 8, 1992, pp. 30–33.
4. Jacob Stein, "Distributed Databases: What Are They, What Are They Good For?" *Journal of Object-Oriented Programming*, Vol. 5, No. 4, July/August 1992, pp. 58–63.
5. Tim Connors and Peter Lyngback, "Providing Uniform Access to Heterogenous Information Bases," *Lecture Notes in Computer Science, Advances in Object-Oriented Database Systems, 2nd International Workshop on Object-Oriented Database Systems,* Springer-Verlag, 1988.
6. Jose A. Blakeley, "DARPA Open Object-Oriented Database Preliminary Module Specification: Object Query Module," Texas Instruments Inc., Version 3, Nov. 25, 1991.

14

The Object Management Group (OMG)

Introduction

This chapter is dedicated to exploring the exciting world of object-oriented software development using distributed databases in a heterogenous environment. The entire chapter is designed to provide a solid introduction to the concept of Object Request Brokers. The Object Management Group's Object Management Architecture is explored in detail to provide the reader with a good understanding of the current state of the industry and of future trends of the technology.

14.1 The Object Management Group (OMG)

The Object Management Group (OMG) is an international software industry consortium, with two primary aims:[1]

(*) Promotion of the object-oriented approach to software engineering in general, and

(*) Development of command models and a common interface for the development and use of large-scale distributed applications (open distributed processing) using object-oriented methodology.

In general, the mission of the OMG is as follows:[2]

1. The OMG is dedicated to maximizing the portability, reusability, and interoperability of software. It is also dedicated to producing a framework and specifications for commercially available object-oriented environments.

2. The OMG provides a Reference Architecture with terms and definitions upon which all specifications are based.

3. The OMG provides an open forum for industry discussion, education, and promotion of OMG-endorsed object technology.

The OMG is not a recognized standards group (like ISO or national bodies such as ANSI and IEEE). It is developing "standards" by means of consensus agreements between member companies leading to a single architecture and interface specification for application and enterprise integration on both the small and large scales. The mission of the OMG can be described as the development of a set of standard interfaces for interoperable software components.

The OMG was founded in April 1989, and continues to have a small, vendor-neutral core staff of seven people. Now comprising about 200 companies, the OMG membership is composed of large and small hardware and software vendors (IBM, Canon, DEC, Phillips, Olivetti, AT&T, Sun Microsystems, Informix, ICL, Enfin Systems, Architecture Projects Management, Apple Computer, O2 Technology, etc.) as well as end-user companies (Citicorp, American Airlines, Royal Bank of Canada, John Deere, etc.) with a common goal: the promotion of open standards for interoperability of applications using an object-oriented framework.

In September 1990, the OMG published the first of its deliverables, the Object Management Architecture (OMA) Guide document. This document outlines a single terminology for object-oriented languages, systems, databases, and application frameworks; an abstract framework for object-oriented systems; a set of both technical and architectural goals; and an architecture (reference model) for distributed applications using object-oriented techniques. To fill out this reference model, the following areas of standardization have been identified:

1. The Object Request Broker, or key communications element, for handling distribution of messages between application objects in a highly interoperable manner

2. The Object Model, or single design-portability abstract model for communicating with OMG-conforming object-oriented systems

3. The Object Services, which will provide the main functions for realizing basic object functionality using the Object Request Broker—the logical modeling and physical storage of objects

4. Interfaces to object-oriented databases

5. An API for common facilities such as spellers, mailers, time managers, etc. The Common Facilities will comprise facilities which are useful in many application domains and which will be made available through OMA compliant class interfaces.

The OMG adoption cycle includes Requests for Information and Proposals, requesting detailed technical and commercial availability information from OMG members about existing products to fill particular parts of the reference model architecture. The OMG Board of Directors have to vote on a technology-by-technology basis while trying to build the standards. The decisions are to be based on both technical and business merit. After passage by technical and business committees to review these responses, the OMG Board of Directors makes a final determination for technology adoption. Adopted specifications are available on a fee-free basis to members and nonmembers alike.

In order to serve OMG membership interested in object-oriented systems arenas besides the distributed system problem, the Group supports Special Interest Groups for discussion of possible standards in other areas. These groups at present are

1. Object-Oriented Databases
2. OO Languages
3. End-User Requirements
4. Parallel Processing
5. Analysis & Design Methodologies
6. Smalltalk
7. Class Libraries

14.2   The Technical Goal of OMG

The goal of the OMG is to specify interface and protocol specifications that help define an OMA that supports interoperable applications based on distributed interoperating objects. The approach is to adopt such specifications from existing technology wherever possible, so as to provide the following:

1. Conformance to the OMG Abstract Object Model, by providing specifications for inheritance of interface, inheritance of implementation, and definition and execution of methods in programs or processes.

2. Transparency of Object Distribution, by providing support for client/server architecture where servers have location transparency and client objects can communicate with server objects without needing to be aware of the specific underlying communication mechanism employed. Object relocation would also be supported.

3. Good performance for local and remote server requests, evaluated in terms of scalability, method invocation time, throughput, etc.

4. Extensibility of systems and ability to dynamically add or change implementations of objects and methods.

5. Support for multiple naming system architectures, and facilitating name spaces in which objects can be named unambiguously

6. Querying facilities based on object names and attributes.

7. Discretionary access control of objects, where the owner of the objects sets access control on objects and metaobjects.

8. Concurrency control for objects.

9. Transaction processing, with support for short and long transactions.

10. Robustness of operations and recovery from failures.

11. Support for versioning of objects and methods, and facilities to update definitions of classes.

12. Notification mechanisms such that objects waiting on specific events can be notified of the occurrence of those events.

13. Conformance to other broadly accepted industry standards.

14.3   The Abstract Object Model

The OMG object model not only provides an organized presentation of the OMG object concepts and terminology, it also defines a computational model for OMG compliant applications and a conceptual framework for OMG proposed technologies.

The OMG object model maintains the distinction between the semantics of objects as perceived by clients of objects and the implementation of those semantics in terms of actual data representations and executable code. Object semantics includes the following:

1. Object creation

2. Object identity

3. Requests and operations on objects

4. Types and signatures

    Object implementation issues include

1. Concepts of methods

2. Data structures

3. Definitions of classes

4. Implementation inheritance

The OMG object model is different from the *classical* object model. In the classical object model, a client sends a message to an object and the object interprets the message to decide which service to perform. The client requesting the service from an object identifies the recipient object and zero or more actual parameters. The OMG proposes a *generalized* object model where a client issues a request that identifies an operation and zero or more parameters, any of which may identify an object. Method selection may be based on any of the objects identified in the request, as well as the operation. This implies that more than one object may be involved in method selection. Thus the classical object model is a special case of the generalized object model proposed by OMG.

14.4   Object Semantics

An OMG object is a combination of an associated state and a set of operations that explicitly embodies an abstraction characterized by the behavior of relevant requests. Objects have clients and provide services to clients. A request to an object is an asynchronous event, and the information associated with a request consists of an operation and zero or more parameters. The operation identifies the service to be performed by objects specified in the parameter list, for the client.

Objects can be unambiguously identified by *handles*. Objects can also be identified by values called *object names*. An object can have multiple handles.

When the requested service is performed, the resulting observable effects are termed "the behavior of a request." The behavior of a request depends on the current state of the object(s) that are the actual parameters of the request as well as the current state of the computational system. The behavior of a request might include generation of other requests.

An object is given an identity to distinguish it from other objects. The object model incorporates the notion of object equivalence; a service could be provided which could compare two values to see if they identify the same object. It should also be possible to support the concept of "merging identity" by causing two distinct objects to become one indistinguishable entity.

Clients making requests can cause objects to be created. The results of such requests can be revealed to the clients by returning a handle to the newly created object back to the client.

Each operation has an associated *signature* that may restrict the possible parameter values that are meaningful in requests that name that operation. A signature is similar in concept to procedure types. Signatures are specified when operations are created.

14.5   Object Implementation

An *object implementation* is a definition of the mechanisms of object creation and the processes by which an object participates in providing an appropriate set of services to clients. The object implementation includes the specification of the data structures used to represent the attributes of the objects and the definitions of the methods that access the data structures. A *class* can be defined as an implementation that can be instantiated to create multiple objects that share the same initial behavior. In general, classes are used to define both an implementation and an interface type.

When a service is requested by a client, a code is executed to perform the service. Such code is termed a *method*. *Binding* is the process of selecting a method to perform a requested service and selecting the data to be accessed by the method. Binding can be static or dynamic. Static binding is handled by compilers during the compilation of the code. Dynamic binding is done by negotiations between the client and the server. The OMG object model does not impose constraints on the process of binding that provide increased predictability for clients. After a method has been selected to perform the requested service, execution may require the copying of data and method from persistent memory to the address space, in a process termed *activation*.

Some object-oriented systems support the notion of object persistence to manage long-lived information about the state of the computation. Object implementations need to consider the issues of object persistence and transience. A persistent object survives the end of the process that created it, and exists until it is explicitly deleted. A transient object, on the other hand, exists as long as it is within the scope of the process or thread that created it.

14.6   The OMG Reference Model

The Reference Model identifies and characterizes the components, interfaces, and protocols that compose OMG's OMA. The details of the Reference Model are evaluated and approved by the OMG by means of technology sponsorship. The Reference Model is responsible for

1. Identifying the major separable components of the OMA

2. Characterizing the functions provided by each OMA component

3. Describing the relationships between OMA components and between OMA components and the operating environment

4. Identifying the protocols and interfaces by which the OMA components can be accessed

It defines

1. Specific objects

2. Specific kinds of objects

3. Specific interfaces to objects

14.7 The Purpose of the OMA Reference Model

The reference model provides a framework for evaluating the distributed object-oriented technology acquired as a result of OMG solicitations. It also expresses OMG's vision of highly interoperable applications and services based on object-oriented technology. It influences the high-level architectural and component designs of specific proposed approaches, and can be used to impose design constraints at the highest architectural level.

The reference model addresses a lot of issues, including the following:

1. The process of making service requests and the process of providing responses to requests

2. The core set of operations that every object should provide

3. The specification of object interfaces incorporating common facilities useful in many applications

14.8 The OMA Overview

The four major components of the OMA are

1. The Object Request Broker (ORB), a component that enables objects to make and receive requests and responses. The ORB is like a switching system, and it helps in routing service requests to the appropriate service objects and in returning responses to the client objects making the requests.

2. Object Services (OS), a component that is responsible for realizing and maintaining objects, which it provides by means of a collection of services with appropriate object interfaces.

3. Common Facilities (CF), a component responsible for general-purpose capabilities useful in many applications, which it provides by means of an appropriate collection of classes and objects.

4. Application Objects (AO), a component that is composed of objects that are specific to particular end-user applications.

The ORB provides the mechanism to connect requests to services and routes the responses to the clients making the requests (see Fig. 14.1). The ORB provides interoperability between applications in a het-

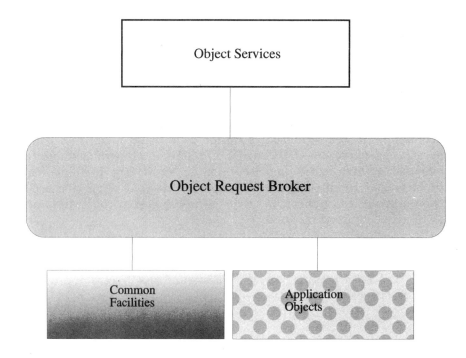

Figure 14.1   OMA model.

erogenous environment. Objects interact by means of requests and the resulting responses. A request is made up of an operation and zero or more parameters. The request results in the invocation of an appropriate method that performs the operation using the parameters, and the results are conveyed to the requester after the operation terminates.

This component of the OMA addresses the standardization of the life cycle management of objects. The life cycle of objects includes the creation of objects, migration or relocation of objects, access control of the objects, and the management of relationship between species of objects. Functions must be provided to perform all these tasks. The Object Services component provides the generic environment in which single objects can perform their tasks.

Object Services, Common Facilities, and Application Objects all communicate using the ORB. The OMA Reference Model does not specify or restrict the way in which the Common Facilities and the Application Objects are structured and implemented.

14.9   The Object Request Broker

The ORB component of the OMA is the communication heart of the standard, and it is designed to guarantee interoperability of objects over a network of heterogenous systems. The ORB serves as a means for software objects running on a network of heterogenous systems to communicate and interact with one another with no knowledge of the hardware and the operating system that the remote object is on.

In late 1991 OMG adopted its first interface technology, for the Object Request Broker portion of the reference model. This technology, adopted from a joint proposal (named "CORBA") of Hewlett-Packard, NCR Corp., HyperDesk Corp., Digital Equipment Corp., Sun Microsystems, and Object Design Inc., includes both static and dynamic interfaces to an interapplication request handling software "bus."

Entities of the OMG system are

- OMG Objects
- Values, e.g. object names and handles
- Operations
- Signatures
- Types

Identifying the need for an ORB, Hagan explains,[2] "A major missing ingredient that prevents object-orientation from promoting true interoperability is a standard that specifies how remote objects interact. This standard would identify the procedures required to locate an object, invoke it, and communicate with it. This is what OMG proposes to do with the Object Request Broker."

The ORB need not be a monolithic component. It can be defined in terms of its interfaces. The ORB interfaces can be organized into the following three categories:[3]

1. Those operations that are the same for all ORB implementations
2. Those operations that are specific to particular types of objects
3. Those operations that are specific to particular styles of object implementations

14.10   Object Services

Object Services are designed to provide basic operations for logical modeling and physical storage of objects. They define a set of intrinsic or root operations that all classes should implement or inherit. These operations are made available through the ORB or some other interface. Object Services provide support for several operations, including the following:[3]

1. Class Management, being able to create, modify, delete, distribute, describe, and control the definitions of classes, interfaces to classes, and relationships between class definitions.

2. Instance Management, being able to modify, delete, copy, move, invoke, and control objects and the relationships between objects.

3. Storage, being able to store large and small objects, including their state and methods, temporarily or permanently.

4. Integrity, being able to ensure the consistency and integrity of object state both within single objects and among objects. This implies support for locking and transactions.

5. Security, being able to provide access constraints at an appropriate level of granularity on objects and their components.

6. Query, being able to select objects or classes from implicitly or explicitly identified collections based on a specified predicate.

7. Versions, the ability to store, correlate, and manage variants of objects.

This is a collection of services that provide basic functions for realizing and maintaining objects. Object Services, along with the ORB, help provide support for distributed object management.

14.11 Common Facilities

Common Facilities provide higher-level services, such as transaction and versioning, that are built using some of the Object Services. Common Facilities can enhance the functionality of operations provided by the Object Services. The Common Facilities provide functions and services via object interfaces. They provide support to the claim that object orientation supports reusability.

The OMG has the ability to make commonly used services available to all clients, thus providing end users uniform semantics that are shared across applications. A service becomes a Common Facility when[3] it

1. Uses the ORB for communication.

2. Implements a facility that the OMG adopts.

3. Has an OMG-compliant object interface.

The following is a list of some Common Facilities:

- Cataloging and browsing of classes and objects
- Link management
- Reusable user interfaces
- Printing and spooling
- Error reporting

- Online help facilities
- Electronic mail

14.12   Application Objects

Objects categorized as Application Objects can provide services for other applications or facilities. Facilities that are commonly used as individual applications in most environments can be integrated into a suite of related applications under the OMA umbrella. While the applications under the Common Facilities are considered standard for OMA-compliant systems, Application Objects need not be standard features, but rather a specialized set of applications that are application-domain specific. For example, a set of CAD applications can be bundled under Application Objects, as can a set of applications that can be used in office automation systems.

14.13   CORBA Specifications

The Common Object Request Broker Architecture (CORBA) describes the architectural structure of the ORB and its components. The major ORB components are

1. The ORB Core
2. The Dynamic Invocation Interface
3. The IDL Stubs Interface
4. The ORB Interface
5. The IDL Skeleton
6. The Object Adapter
7. The Interface Repository

An ORB may be configured in a variety of ways. The actual implementation is left to the vendor.

1. Client- and implementation-resident ORB: The ORB can be implemented in the client and the object implementations rather than as a separate external entity.
2. Server-based ORB: The ORB can be incorporated into a server or based as an application on a server. Clients and implementations can communicate with one or more such servers, which are responsible for routing requests from clients to implementations.
3. System-based ORB: The ORB can be incorporated into the operating system, in which case its functionality would be just an addi-

tional service of an operating system, albeit with security, robustness, and performance.

Object definitions are presented to the ORB upon request in one of two forms:

1. By incorporating the information procedurally into stub routines

2. As objects accessed through the dynamically accessible Interface Repository

14.14   The ORB Core

The ORB Core helps client objects communicate with the server objects. Client applications can make requests to a server object, and the ORB Core communicates the request. Similarly, responses from the server object to requests from clients are communicated back to the clients by the ORB Core. There are no direct client or server interfaces to the ORB Core. Functional details of the ORB Core are not precise, as they can be implemented different on different networks and operating systems. CORBA is designed to support different object mechanisms, and it does so by structuring the ORB with components above the ORB Core, which provide interfaces that can mask the differences between ORB Cores.

The clients and the server objects can both communicate with the ORB Core using the ORB Interface. This enables them to take advantage of the services provided by the ORB Core.

14.15   Client Interfaces to the ORB Core: IDL and the Dynamic Invocation

The client interfaces to the ORB Core are provided by the Dynamic Invocation Interface and the static Interface Definition Language (IDL) Stubs. The IDL is an extension of the C++ programming language. It enables the software developer designing an object to specify the object's interface to the ORB. Client applications generally approach the objects and the ORB interfaces through the perspective of a language mapping, bringing the ORB right up to the programming level. After the creation of an object, its signature is declared using the IDL. Declaring the signature involves declaring its inheritance, attributes, and procedural operators. Using the IDL compiler, the call stubs that the client calls are created. The IDL compiler also creates the calling skeleton to invoke the remote object.

The IDL compiler also creates header files that can be compiled with the client's application code to declare the interface procedures. These header files can be used in C or C++ code. At run time, the

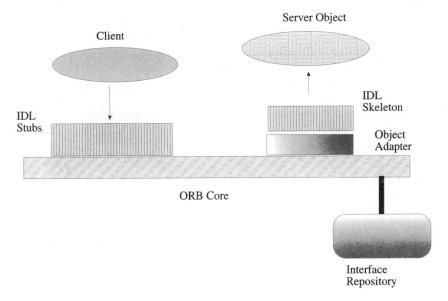

Figure 14.2 Client communicating with server object using ORB and IDL stubs.

client application invokes the possibly remote server object by calling the object's IDL specified stubs. The ORB Core gets the request and transmits it to the IDL skeleton, where the server object's methods are invoked on behalf of the client (Fig. 14.2).

A similar procedure is available for dynamic invocation (see Fig. 14.3). In this case, the client object has to inform the ORB Core as to its intentions. The ORB Core needs to know the intended receiver of the client's request, the parameters that need to be passed, and the results expected. To facilitate the specification of such information, the ORB Core provides a set of procedures. The client then invokes a sequence of ORB procedures to provide the required information about the desired server object and the parameters. The ORB Core takes this information and looks up the server object in the Interface Repository. This is similar to a directory lookup. The Interface Repository tells the ORB where the server object is located, and how to invoke it. To invoke the server object's methods, the Object Adapter is used. To allow for dynamic invocation, the implementor of the server object must declare invocation information to the ORB to be deposited in the ORB Interface Repository.

A client using the dynamic invocation interface to send a request to an object obtains the same semantics as a client using the operation stub generated from the type specification. A request is usually made up of the following:

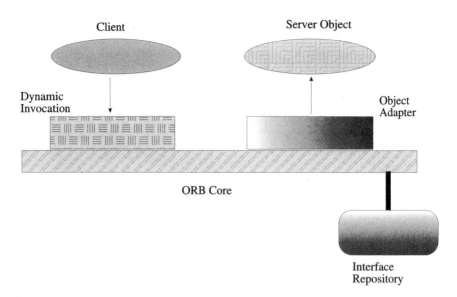

Figure 14.3   Dynamic invocation of server object by client.

1. An object reference

2. An operation

3. A list of parameters

The parameters are presented in a list. Each parameter is presented in its native data form. When the request is invoked, parameters are subjected to run-time type checking. The parameters must be in the same order as the parameters defined for the operation in the Interface Repository.

14.16   The IDL Compiler

When the IDL compiler compiles a user-specified interface code, it generates the skeleton code and client stubs for the ORB, and header files with prototypes for the client to include in the application code (see Fig. 14.4). Compile-time type checking occurs with the IDL invocation method, since the stub that the client calls is declared in a header file. In the case of dynamic invocation, it is not possible to have this extra level of error checking.

14.17   Object Adapter

An Object Adapter exports a public interface to the object implementation and a private interface to the skeleton. It provides a primary

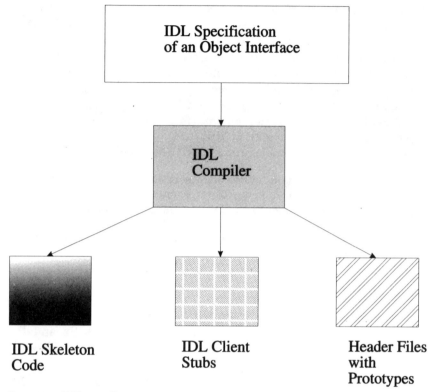

Figure 14.4 IDL compiler.

means by which an object implementation can access the ORB services. The Object Adapter is usually built on a private ORB-dependent interface.

Object Adapters are responsible for the following operations:[3]

1. Generation and interpretation of object references

2. Method invocation

3. Security of interactions

4. Object and implementation activation and deactivation

5. Mapping object references to the corresponding object implementation

6. Registration of implementations

Some of these operations may actually be done by the ORB Core on behalf of the Adapter. The object implementation may rely on a set of services provided by an Adapter. If the ORB Core provides the functionality, the Adapter might just act as an interface to the ORB Core. If the object implementation is moved to another environment where the ORB Core does not provide the required functionality, the Adapter will have to provide the necessary features to the object implementation. Thus, with an Object Adapter, it is possible for an object implementation to have access to a service whether or not it is implemented in the ORB Core—if the ORB Core provides the service, the Adapter simply provides an interface for it; if not, the Adapter must implement it on top of the ORB Core.

Anderson[4] has suggested using an OODBMS for an Object Adapter:

> With some modifications to the ORB specification, an OODBMS can be a more efficient Object Adapter for large numbers of small objects. The Object Adapter defined in the ORB model uses RPCs for object-client communication and thus is more suited to handling large objects such as whole spreadsheets or documents. Invoking an RPC for each object in a CAD drawing can totally obliterate the OODBMS' native performance.

14.18 The ORB Interface

It is possible to go directly to the ORB for some services using the ORB Interface. The ORB Interface is the same for all ORBs, and does not depend on the object's interface or the Object Adapter. The ORB Core provides access to its services mostly through the Object Adapter, the client stubs, and the skeletons, or by means of the dynamic invocation mechanism. Thus, there are very few services that it needs to provide through the ORB Interface. There are only a few operations that are common across all objects, and they are useful to both clients and implementations of objects.

14.19 The Interface Repository

This is a service that provides persistent objects representing the IDL information at run time to other services in the ORB. The ORB uses the information from the Interface Repository to perform requests from clients to object implementations. Using the information in the Interface Repository, it is possible for a program to encounter an object whose interface was not known at compile time, yet be able to determine what operations are valid on the object and make an invocation on it. The Interface Repository is also used to store other kinds of information, such as debugging information, libraries of stubs or skeletons, etc.

When a request from a client provides values associated with the request, the ORB needs access to the object definitions stored in the Interface Repository to interpret the values. This is done to

1. Provide type checking of request signatures.

2. Assist in checking the correctness of interface inheritance graphs.

3. Assist in providing interoperability between different ORB implementations.

The Interface Repository can also be used to

1. Manage the installation and distribution of interface definitions.

2. Provide components of a CASE environment.

3. Provide interface information to language bindings.

4. Provide components of end-user environments.

As part of the interface definitions of objects, the Interface Repository manages the following collection of interface objects:[3]

1. Repository: contains constants, typedefs, exceptions, interface definitions, and modules

2. ModuleDef: a logical grouping of interfaces

3. InterfaceDef: an interface definition

4. AttributeDef: the definition of an attribute of the interface

5. OperationDef: the definition of an operation on the interface

6. ParameterDef: the definition of an argument to an operation

7. TypeDef: the definition of named type that is not an interface

8. ConstantDef: the definition of a named constant

9. ExceptionDef: the definition of an exception that can be raised by an operation

14.20   The IDL

IDL (the Interface Definition Language) is the language that can be used by clients to describe the interfaces associated with the objects they intend to call. Client applications are written not in the IDL but in other programming languages for which mappings from IDL concepts have been defined. Initially, only the C language bindings of IDL concepts were made available by OMG. Other language bindings are expected to follow.

The IDL grammar has syntax similar to C++. It follows the same lexical rules. It is, however, more restrictive than C++. Some of the restrictions are

1. A function return type is mandatory.

2. A name must be supplied with each formal parameter to an operation declaration.

3. Integer types cannot be defined simply as an int or unsigned; they must be declared explicitly as short or long.

14.21   Commercial ORB Products

The CORBA specification was assembled from specifications submitted by DEC, HyperDesk, NCR, Object Design, and jointly by HP and Sun, in response to a request for proposals (RFP) issued by OMG. All of these submitting companies plan to release their own version of an ORB, compliant with the CORBA specifications. ORBs are likely to become important components of most networking environments, and may make it significantly easier for programmers to access networked services, such as printers and databases, on remote systems.

HyperDesk has developed its HY-DOM product in "strict compliance" with the OMG ORB standard. DEC has developed an OMG-compliant Application Control Architecture to link office automation and other applications. SunSoft, in cooperation with Hewlett-Packard, has developed the Distributed Object Environment, an OMG-compliant infrastructure. Several other OMG-compliant systems are expected in the next few years.

References

1. Jim Truitt, "Re: RFI: Object Management Group," Article in comp.object, Message-ID: <1992Aug27.180311.26030@mlb.semi.harris.com>, 27 Aug 92.
2. Tom Hagan, "The Promise of the ORB Spec," *Open Systems Today,* March 2, 1992, pp. 51–54.
3. OMG, "The Common Object Request Broker: Architecture and Specification," OMG Document Number 91.12.1, Revision 1.1, 1991.
4. Julie Anderson, "Data Management," Editorial on Development Tools, *Open Systems Today,* March 16, 1992, p. 24.

15

OODBMS Products

Introduction

In this chapter, various OODBMSs not covered in the previous chapters will be briefly explored—GemStone, Iris, and UniSQL. This chapter is designed to provide a flavor of some popular OODBMSs that might help put the field of OODBMSs in perspective.

15.1 GemStone

GemStone was developed to meet not only the needs of the engineering markets but also those of the commercial and MIS markets. It emphasizes robustness, active objects, multiple language support, and easy-to-use tools. GemStone has been designed with an evolutionary approach to federated distribution, high availability, and scalability.

15.1.1 GemStone architecture

The basic components of the GemStone architecture are

1. The Gem server process

2. The Stone monitor

The Gem server is where the object behavior specified using the data manipulation language (DML) is executed. The server has both the object cache and the page cache. Queries are evaluated at the server. Object identifiers are allocated by the Stone monitor. The Stone monitor coordinates commits with the Gem server, and the server is responsible for committing transactions.

The databases can span multiple volumes the component of each database stored on a single disk volume is referred to as an extent.

GemStone allows multiple extents in a database. The ability to distribute database replicates across the network aids in recovery from processor failure. If a processor failure occurs, the machine on which the replicate resides can assume the functionality that resided on the failed processor. To support replicates and remote servers, GemStone uses a page server process that implements a subset of NFS functionality.

GemStone employs an optimistic concurrency control. It also uses an object locking protocol that guarantees an application that there will be no concurrency conflict on objects by presenting a locked object to other transactions as though it had been read or written at the time the lock was acquired. An object cache is used for objects created by a transaction. A page cache is used for objects that are accessed from the database.

15.1.2 GemStone interfaces

GemStone supports multiple languages and tools. It provides a library of C functions to provide access to the database structurally and by sending messages. Database schema and objects are stored in the GemStone object server. GemStone also provides a C++ interface, and persistent objects stored in the database by the C++ interface can be accessed by interfaces employing other languages. Applications can either link to the C++ interface or communicate with it using RPCs. Class definitions are stored in the database using a utility called *registrar*. The C++ interface maintains a hash table of the location within virtual memory of C++ objects managed by GemStone. The table is indexed by object identifiers.

Objects belonging to the classes registered with GemStone can be accessed in the following two ways, using two distinct types of pointers:[1]

1. GPointers are object identifiers and are transparently dereferenced via the hash table.

2. DPointers (direct pointers) point directly to the virtual memory location of objects.

A GPointer can be converted into a DPointer, and when this happens, the object's location within virtual memory is pinned, thus assuring the validity of the DPointer.

15.1.3 GeODE

Servio Logic also provides a software development environment for GemStone, called the GemStone Object Development Environment,

GeODE. GeODE provides a *visual programming* environment for the development of interactive object-oriented software based on GemStone. A visual program is a graphical representation of a procedure to be performed on the data being held by a form or field, or on the form or field itself. Visual programs are good for[2]

- Getting data from a field or form
- Performing operations on the data
- Putting data into a field or form
- Performing operations on fields and forms themselves
- Specifying the sequence of data acquisition and transformation

Triggers can be set for the visual programs. Setting triggers involves choosing the events which will trigger program execution. When setting triggers, it is important not to cause infinite loops.

15.2   The IRIS Database System

The IRIS database system was developed at Hewlett-Packard to meet the needs of new applications such as office automation, engineering databases, knowledge-based systems, etc., that require a new set of capabilities and features not currently present in conventional database systems. IRIS addresses the following issues:[3]

1. Rich data modeling constructs
2. Direct database support for inference
3. Nonconventional data types, such as images, audio, video, text, etc.
4. Lengthy interactions with the database, spanning minutes to many days
5. Multiple versions of data

The IRIS DBMS was designed to meet these needs. To address all such issues, the IRIS DBMS has been designed around the architecture shown in Fig. 15.1. The IRIS database system relies on relational algebra as its theory of computation.

15.2.1   The IRIS architecture

Central to the IRIS architecture is the concept of the Object Manager, which is responsible for the query and update facilities of the DBMS. The Storage Manager provides associative access and update capabilities to a single relation at a time. It also provides support for transactions.

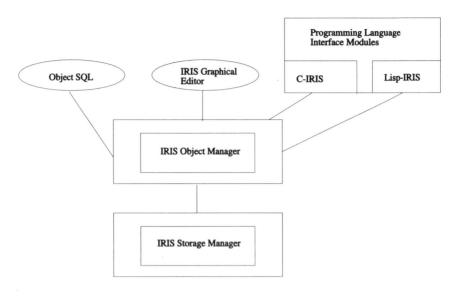

Figure 15.1   The IRIS architecture.

The IRIS data model is based on the following three kinds of con-structs:

1. Objects
2. Types
3. Functions

Objects in IRIS represent entities and concepts from the applica-tion domain. *Literal* objects are objects such as integers, strings, lists, etc. that are identified by their contents. *Surrogate* objects are those corresponding to real-world objects, and are represented by a system-generated *object identifier,* or *oid.* Collections of objects that are capa-ble of participating in a definable set of activities are termed *types.* Types have unique names. The activities of types are modeled by *functions.* IRIS supports a *type hierarchy.* Surrogate objects may belong to multiple types, even if the types are not related by a sub-type/supertype relationship.

Using these three kinds of constructs, the IRIS data model supports the following features:

1. Inheritance
2. Generic properties
3. Constraints

4. Complex or nonnormalized data

5. User-defined functions

6. Version control

7. Inference

8. Extensible data types

Each object in IRIS has an assigned, system-wide, unique object identifier, or OID. This facilitates referential integrity. Objects can be manipulated only by means of functions. Objects are classified by types, and objects belonging to the same type share common functions. A function may be applied to an object only if the function is defined on a type to which the object belongs. Properties of IRIS objects are modeled by functions.

There are three interactive interfaces to the database:

1. A driver for the Object Manager interface

2. Object SQL (OSQL), an OO extension to SQL

3. The Graphical Editor

15.2.2   The IRIS Object Manager

The IRIS Object Manager provides support for the following:

1. Schema definition

2. Data manipulation

3. Query processing

The Object Manager provides primitives for explicit creation and deletion of nonliteral objects. It also provides primitives for assigning and updating values to their functions. To support referential integrity, when an object is deleted, all references to that object are also deleted.

15.2.3   The Storage Manager

The IRIS Storage Manager is built on top of a conventional relational storage manager. Tables can be created and dropped at any time. The HP-SQL system currently being used as the core of the Storage Manager supports transactions with savepoints, restores with savepoints, concurrency control, logging and recovery, archiving, indexing, and buffer management. Since it is a relational system, it provides tuple-at-a-time processing with commands to perform CRUD (Create, Retrieve, Update, Delete) type operations. The basic function of the Storage Manager is to retrieve tuples from tables.

The Storage Manager supports *long fields,* which are fields with field lengths that exceed the page size of 4K bytes. Long fields are assigned a unique identifier by the IRIS Storage Manager. The data in the long fields can be retrieved and updated, and subsets of the long field data can also be accessed. Each long field will have an associated list of tuples which reference it. This list helps maintain referential integrity.

15.2.4   Functions and rules in IRIS

Functions are used to express

1. Attributes of objects

2. Relationships between objects

3. Computations on objects

Functions are defined over types. They may be multivalued. A type can be characterized by the collections of functions defined over it. Functions are declared by specifying a name with its argument and result types. The implementation of functions is determined by the user, and can be one of the following:

1. Stored functions: Functions are stored in persistent data structures, which can be tablelike structures similar to those employed in relational databases.

2. Derived functions: Functions can be derived from other functions. A derived function can have side effects. They support associative access to sets of objects.

3. Foreign functions: These are programs written in some programming language and compiled outside to IRIS. The object code is stored in IRIS, and it is dynamically loaded and executed when the function is invoked.

The Storage Manager is capable of evaluating derived and foreign functions in order to retrieve tuples from the database.

Rules are modeled as IRIS functions. IRIS supports conjunctive, disjunctive, and nonrecursive rules.

15.2.5   The IRIS Object SQL interface

The IRIS Object Manager supports the atomic level of operations for the objects. The Object SQL interface combines this concept of an atomic object with the set of property functions that the user considers to be intrinsic to the nature of the object. A functional style of

Extensions to SQL:

1. Users manipulate types and functions rather than tables.

2. Objects may be referenced directly rather than indirectly, through their keys. Interface variables may be bound to objects on creation or retrieval and may then be used to refer to the objects in subsequent statements.

3. User-defined functions and IRIS system functions may appear in where and select clauses to give concise and powerful retrieval.

Figure 15.2 The IRIS Object SQL interface.

interface is adopted for expressing the relationships among interconnected objects. Object SQL is treated as a potential evolutionary growth path for SQL. See Fig. 15.2.

The IRIS Storage Manager is responsible for providing associative access and update capabilities to a single relation at a time. It is also responsible for transactions. The OSQL commands can be embedded in programming languages supported by IRIS. The traditional arguments for embedding query languages also apply to OSQL. However, the "impedance mismatch" problem traditionally faced by embedded languages is overcome by employing user-defined types provided by the object model, since they can be used to pass information between host and the embedded languages.

15.3 UniSQL

UniSQL tries to merge the best of both the relational and object-oriented worlds. It is an attempt to seamlessly unite relational and OO technology. It can be considered to be a relational DBMS with extensive OO extensions which differentiate it from any other current DBMS. UniSQL is not the only vendor trying to bridge the gap between relational and OO databases. Several relational DBMS vendors have attempted to do just that. Triggers and stored procedures are supported by several relational databases. Some relational DBMSs provide support for user-defined data types. Most of the relational databases provide support for binary large objects, called BLOBS. UniSQL does not just try to extend the relational technology, but tries to capture much of the object-oriented theory by implementing it in UniSQL.

UniSQL/X has incorporated the OO concepts of inheritance, composition, methods, and arbitrary data types to meet the following goals:[4]

1. Improve data modeling capability

2. Increase data integrity

3. Improve performance

4. Increase maintainability

5. Increase usability

6. Increase productivity

15.3.1 Table inheritance

Tables in UniSQL are treated like classes. Thus, tables can be subclasses of other tables, and a subclass inherits the fields and procedures associated with the table that is at the higher levels in the hierarchy. Thus, the concepts of supertypes and subtypes can be incorporated into the relational data model.

The UniSQL/X Database Management System extends the relational model and ANSI SQL language with support for unstructured data types and object-oriented concepts such as encapsulation and multiple inheritance. The database has built-in transaction management and query optimization features.

UniSQL is not yet a mature product. It will be a few years before the industry can decide on such products.

References

1. Paul Butterworth, Allen Otis, and Jacob Stein, "The GemStone Object Database Management System," *Communications of the ACM,* vol. 34, no. 10, 1991, pp. 64–77.
2. Servio Corporation, "GeODE Release Notes," Beta-4 Release for the SPARCstation, September 1992.
3. D. H. Fishman et al., "Overview of the IRIS DBMS," Technical Report HPL-SAL-89-15, Hewlett-Packard Company, Jan. 10, 1989.
4. Richard Finkelstein, "UniSQL Merges Relational and Object-Oriented Models," an independent study by Performance Computing, Inc., commissioned by UniSQL, Inc., January 1992.

16

Research in OODB

Introduction

This chapter explores current research trends in OODBMSs. The concepts covered in this chapter include rules, constraints, active OODBs, and capabilities.

16.1   Research in DBMS

Researchers in DBMS have explored interoperability, distributed systems, multidatabase environments, query optimizations, and several other areas in the last two decades. Several approaches to locking, concurrency control, recovery, and transactional semantics have been aggressively pursued and studied. DBMS technology has matured, and the focus of DBMS research has shifted to other related fields.

16.2   Active Object-Oriented Databases

Active databases are those in which changes in the state of specific data trigger the execution of some related operation. A timely response to critical situations is necessary in some applications, and this is typically provided by monitoring conditions defined on states of specific database data; once these conditions occur, specific actions are invoked, subject to some timing constraints.

Active databases are databases that respond automatically to events generated internally or externally to the system itself, without any user intervention. The nature of the response is arbitrary, and depends on the application semantics. The desired behavior is commonly specified by production rules, which are predicate-action pairs to be triggered at specific events.

Active databases can be used to provide a lot of the same functionality found in conventional databases, in addition to providing mechanisms for implementing timing requirements and consistency constraints over the shared database. Dayal et al. have proposed an approach in which triggers and rules are considered as first-class objects, making it possible for rules to have their own attributes and providing the flexibility of rules being related to or associated with objects. Rules can be considered to be an entity type. Dayal et al. have proposed the following structure for rules:[1]

Rule identifier	Like any other entity, each rule has a unique entity identifier
Event	The event causes the system to fire the rule. Typed formal arguments may be defined for the event; these are bound to actual arguments when the rule fires.
Condition	The coupling mode between the triggering transaction and the condition evaluation, and a collection of queries to be evaluated when the rule is fired.
Action	The coupling mode between the condition evaluation and the action execution, and an operation to be executed when the rule is fired and the condition is satisfied.
Timing constraints	Deadlines, priorities/urgencies, or value functions.
Contingency plans	Alternative actions to be executed in case the timing constraints cannot be met.
Attributes	Additional properties of rules (may yield scalar values such as strings and integers, or complex entities that may themselves have attributes).

16.3   The HiPAC System

The HiPAC (High-Performance ACtive database system) project combined active database management and timing constraints in order to provide contingency plans, which are alternative actions that can be executed when the system discovers that it cannot complete the task in time. The HiPAC provides five main functional components:[2]

Object manager: It provides object-oriented data management.

Transaction manager: It is responsible for the nested transaction model.

Event detectors: They are responsible for detecting and reporting primitive events (database operations, temporal or application-defined events) to the rule manager.

Rule manager: It is responsible for mapping events to the rule firing, and rule firing to transactions.

Condition evaluator: It determines which rule conditions are satisfied.

Events are detected by the event manager and reported to the rule manager, which then decides which of the rules should be fired. The rule manager then calls in the transaction manager to create a transaction for the condition evaluator. The condition evaluator is called to evaluate the rule's condition. This can result in the creation of a transaction, by the transaction manager, for the action that should be executed.

Rules are treated as first-class objects in HiPAC. Every rule is an instance of a rule object class. Rules can be related to other objects and can also have attributes. In addition, rule objects can be locked, fired, enabled, and disabled.

16.4 Rules in O_2

The O_2 rules system is integrated into the O_2 DBMS. Rules are implemented as objects. They are also treated like any other schema component. Temporal lists of rules are maintained, and when a rule is executed, the temporal lists of the rules are rearranged. Rule objects in O_2 are independent of any application, and rules can be updated or deleted. The rule objects differ slightly from other kinds of objects in that O_2 rule objects can be disabled and enabled. When an event occurs, the related rule is activated and its condition is checked, and if the condition is satisfied, a related action is executed.

In general, rule objects in O_2 are tuples of the form[3]

```
< Name, E, Q, A, P, S, AP >
```

where

Name is a string identifying the rule.

E(vent) is an expression describing one event which triggers rule verification.

Q(uery) is an O_2 query. It contains the predicate to be tested in order to execute the action.

A(ction) is a sequence of CO_2 operations and corresponds to the action to be performed if the condition is met.

P(riority) is an integer that ranks the rule, to be used when there is more than a rule applicable for a given event.

S(tatus) indicates whether the rule is enabled or disabled.

AP(plicability) indicates when to check the rule, e.g. pre- or post-method execution.

The `Rule` built-in class serves as a base class from which other rule classes can be derived. The update operations on rules are Add, Delete, Enable, Disable, Fire, and Change_priority.

16.5   Integrity Maintenance Using Constraints in O₂

Static integrity constraints are used to ensure consistency of a database. Two-state predicate constraints have been used to express a type of dynamic constraints, by specifying the initial and final states of a transaction. In general, dynamic integrity constraints are predicates specified over a sequence of states. First-order logic can be used to express static constraints, while temporal logic can be employed to express dynamic constraints.

The constraint maintenance mechanism in O_2 takes advantage of the production rule subsystem, which is a general rule mechanism. Each constraint is transformed into a set of special objects, called rules, which will monitor integrity. Thus, object integrity is made into a responsibility of the objects themselves. Integrity enforcement, in O_2, employs rules which are activated when selected events take place. It is ensured by performing compensating actions, determined by database and application semantics. Constraints are thus enforced by means of O_2 production rules, which are predicate-action pairs to be triggered by specific actions.

Constraints can be inherited by subclasses, i.e., a constraint defined for a given class is automatically enforced in all its subclasses. Constraints can be created, inserted, modified, or deleted at will, independent of any application.

16.6   Integrating OOP Paradigm and Rule-Based Programming Paradigm

The LOGRES project addressed extended database systems that are based on the integration of the object-oriented data modeling paradigm and the rule-based approach for the specification of queries and updates.[4] The LOGRES data model, being based on an OOP approach, supports the concepts of classes of objects, generalization hierarchies, and object sharing. Integrity constraints are used to verify the consistency of legal database states, and they are expressed using the standard rule-based programming language. The user language is rule-based. It extends Datalog to support sets, multisets, sequences, and controlled forms of negation.

The LOGRES database includes classes and associations. The schema is expressed by type equations. Objects are given an object-id (OID). The OIDs are generated and managed by the system, not by the users. The OIDs provide for object sharing. The associations are sets of tuples. Associations include classes, while the reverse is not true. The OIDs of objects are included within tuples of associations. Thus tuples can be considered to be collections of attributes and OIDs.

The classes are used to provide the concept of object sharing and inheritance. The associations provide conventional and NF2 relations to the model. The results of user queries are usually associations. Associations cannot contain other associations. LOGRES has strong typing and allows static type checking. It also permits the separation of the notions of instance and schema, as in the relational model.

16.7   LAURE

LAURE is an efficient and extensible object-oriented language. It is a "pure" object-oriented language where everything is an object. LAURE is also a reflective language.

LAURE can be used for logic programming, since it is based on LISP. LAURE supports the semantics of sets. It also emphasizes the relational aspect inherent in any object-oriented language. It can be used for knowledge representation, by employing the set/relation scheme. LAURE can also be used to express deductive rules. These rules can be expressed by means of the logic language support in LAURE. The deductive rules can then be converted into demon programs that can be compiled into C functions.

LAURE is an interpretive language. LAURE programs can also be compiled. The three representation of sets in LAURE are

Lists

Lattice_sets

Selections

Each list, lattice_set, or selection represents a set. SET is the set of all sets in LAURE. It is the union of LATTICE_SET, LIST, and SELECTION.

A list structure and its enumeration can represent a set—for example, the list (John Smith Joe) and its enumeration {John, Smith, Joe}.

A lattice_set represents the union of all its subsets and its sets of instances. A lattice set that has only instances can be represented as

```
OFFICE_FURNITURE = {Table, Chair, Desk}
```

LAURE supports the standard operations on objects, but extends the object model into an entity-relationship model by allowing the attachment of methods and relations to types, which expand the notion of classes to include any arbitrary set expressions involving other classes (types), as well as sets of individual objects.[5] LAURE supports logical rules and constraints, which are defined as objects, and offers a deductive engine that takes advantage of the object-oriented nature of the rules and constraints.

16.8 The ACOOD System

The ACOOD (ACtive Object-Oriented Database system) is an experimental OODBMS developed at University of Skovde. It is an active database system based on Ontos, a commercial OODBMS. Berndtsson[2] has provided the following requirements definition for active database systems:

1. An object-oriented DBMS that can provide object-oriented data management.
2. Support for persistent classes and user-defined access methods.
3. Support for nested transactions. This requirement is due to the active database system's ability to cater for nested rule firing.
4. Support for representing rules and invoking user-defined procedures, so that the actions associated with the rules can be executed.
5. A module responsible for detecting and reporting events.
6. A module that can evaluate and determine if a rule's condition part is satisfied.
7. A module responsible for firing the appropriate rules in a correct manner, according to event and possible rules conflict.

16.9 Objects in Distributed Systems

The term *distributed systems* (DS) is typically defined as a system that consists of multiple processors which do not share primary memory (multiprocessors) and which communicate using a message-passing mechanism over the network. Programming in distributed systems is rather complicated, and a number of issues are usually encountered, some of which are listed below:

- Location of the entities
- Migration of entities
- Location transparency
- Support for parallelism
- Message-passing mechanisms for communication
- Synchronization of activities

- Data sharing

The impact of OOT on distributed systems is not yet clearly understood. A lot more research needs to be focused on the application of OO concepts to solve the problems in DS. Both OOT and DS employ the client/server model to model the behavior of client entities and server entities. The client/server model usually incorporates a message-passing mechanism for communication between the client and the server. Services in a DS can be viewed as being encapsulated within a server which implements a well-defined interface through which the other entities in the system that are clients can access the service. This encapsulation is akin to encapsulation in objects.

Hutchison and Walpole[6] have claimed that the object model is more powerful and flexible as a system structuring construct than the client/server model.

> Distributed entities can be modeled as user-defined typed objects. The type of an operation specifies the operations which can be performed on it. Therefore, if the type of an object is known, it is possible to determine its interface. In addition, the object model uses a message passing paradigm and does not require that communication semantics match those of a procedure call. Asynchronous communications may be adopted, giving scope for the increased use of concurrency. Therefore, as a communication model, it is more flexible than the remote procedure call model.

16.10 Object-Oriented Distributed Systems

The application of OO concepts to solve the problems in DS has attracted a lot of researchers. OOP makes more powerful language concepts available for DS design. A DS can be considered to be composed of a number of cooperating objects that are located on separate nodes. Objects can serve as the unit of distribution in the DS. Several strategies can be employed to map objects onto processors. The location of objects on the network can be statically defined or dynamically computed, and can be under the control of the programmer or determined by the system. It is also possible to provide location transparency.

It is possible, using appropriate OOT, to provide some degree of parallelism in the objects. For example, it should be possible to allow clients to send messages to several server objects at the same time, and to allow clients to proceed in parallel with the objects that receive their messages. If objects can concurrently handle multiple clients, they must contain some mechanism to control concurrent access to shared data.

The presence of class hierarchies and the distribution transparency brings up the issue of distributed inheritance. The interaction between an object and its corresponding class or superclasses can be a problem, especially in Smalltalk-based systems. Forcing objects to reside only on the same nodes as their classes and superclasses severely restricts object mobility and object migration.

The Advanced Networked Systems Architecture (ANSA) project in the U.K. has tried to address some of the issues that are generally encountered by the combination of OOT and DS. ANSA researchers have identified six types of transparencies that are useful in distributed OO systems:

- *Access transparency:* Local and remote services are accessed in the same way.

- *Location transparency:* The user need not know the whereabouts of a service.

- *Migration transparency:* If a service location moves, this is not apparent to the user.

- *Replication transparency:* If there are several replicated services, the user is not aware of this.

- *Concurrency transparency:* If there are several users accessing a service concurrently, each user is unaware of the others.

- *Fault transparency:* The presence of a fault is hidden from the user.

16.11   More about Capabilities

The basic idea of capabilities is that access to objects is controlled by the ownership and presentation of capabilities. Programs can access only those objects for which they possess a capability. For security reasons, a capability for an object should be obtained only by creating a new object or by receiving a capability from another program.

In general, capabilities have three components.[7] These are a unique name identifying the object, a set of access rights, and some status information. Although the ownership of a capability guarantees the right to access the corresponding object, the access rights field may restrict the level of access allowed. When a capability is presented in order to access an object, the system has to check that the type of access does not exceed that specified in the capability. Status information indicates which operations can be performed on the capability itself. For example, a *no copy* bit can help restrict the copying capability, possibly on a user basis.

It must be possible to revoke access to objects using the capability system.

16.12   The Next Generation of OODBMS Applications

The next generation database applications will try to provide for the storage and retrieval of vast amounts of data that are highly complex. Examples of such data can be found in satellite images and astronomical data. There is no easy technique for storing such vast amounts of information. Thus, there is no easy technique for searching through such data.

A typical CAD/CAM and Engineering Data Management System has the following requirements:

- It needs to handle complex and intelligent data types such as constraint representations, manufacturing assemblies, project plans, and solid models with topology and tolerances.

- Customers' applications may have large sets of linked data—some Bill of Materials applications, some with millions of parts to be stored in the database.

The next generation DBMSs will have to provide facilities for such systems. Other types of applications might involve the integration of systems that are quite disjoint and independent today. A good example would be the integration of data and maps on roads stored by a highway department with maps and charts of underground phone cables owned and operated by a local phone company. Such an integrated database system must maintain and integrate information about repairs and construction projects from the viewpoints of hundreds of subcontractors.

The research on DNA sequence by the human genome project is likely to create vast amounts of information and images. After the genes have been charted, using the collected data to diagnose diseases will require a new technology of information storage and retrieval.

The emerging technologies such as multimedia are likely to introduce several new kinds of data, and with them, newer storage and retrieval requirements. Next generation DBMS applications will require a new set of services in different areas:[8]

1. There will be new kinds of data, probably large and internally complex. A new type of query language might be required for large data.

2. Type management is going to be important.

3. Rules are likely to be common. They can be *declarative* or *imperative*. Rules may include elaborate constraints that the designer wants enforced.

4. They will require new concepts not found in most current applications—spatial data, time, uncertainty.

5. Scaling up to the next order of magnitude in terms of size. Building an index dynamically on terabytes of information is not practical. Making a dump of such a large database might not be feasible even in case of hardware failures.

6. Ad hoc queries might take a long time to execute. Parallelism might be a solution. Users' queries would probably need to be executed at nearly linear speedup.

7. Tertiary storage and long-duration transactions may be necessary. Part of the data being processed may still be in archives. Thus, query optimization will be critical, and movement of data between storage media will have to be minimized.

8. Support for multiple versions and configurations will be necessary.

9. Databases are likely to operate in heterogenous and distributed environments. It may be possible to create a single worldwide database system from which users can obtain information on any topic covered by data, made available by purveyors, and on which business can be transacted in a uniform way.

10. Uniform browsing capability that can be applied to any one of individual databases. The ability to interrogate the structure of the database is imperative if browsing is to be supported across several databases.

11. In a multidatabase system, the definition of data may not be consistent across all databases, leading to answers that may not be semantically consistent. Future interoperability of databases will require dramatic progress to be made on semantic issues.

12. Mediators, a class of information sources that stand between the user and the heterogenous databases, will be needed to address the problems of semantic inconsistencies and database merging.

13. Name services may need to be globally accessible, with mechanisms by which items enter and leave such name servers.

14. Security, especially in a distributed and heterogeneous environment, might be a big problem. Good authentication services will be necessary for reliable identification of subjects making database access.

15. Site scale-up issues must be addressed, and this might involve design of better algorithms for query processing, concurrency control, and replication.

16. Transactions in a large distributed, heterogenous environment are a difficult issue, and will have to be supported. If each local database employs a different concurrency control mechanism, integrating such systems so as to provide uniform transaction semantics will be a problem.

The next-generation database applications will have tremendous challenges, and will require new capabilities. These new capabilities might force researchers to rethink algorithms for almost all DBMS operations.

References

1. Umeshwar Dayal, Alejandro P. Buchmann, and Dennis R. McCarthy, "Rules Are Objects Too: A Knowledge Model for an Active, Object-Oriented Database System," *Lecture Notes in Computer Science, Advances in Object-Oriented Database Systems, 2nd International Workshop on Object-Oriented Database Systems,* Springer-Verlag, 1988.
2. Mikael Berndtsson, "ACOOD: An Approach to an Active Object-Oriented DBMS," Ph.D. thesis, Department of Computer Science, University of Skovde, 1991.
3. Bauzer Claudia Medeiros and Patrick Pfeffer, "Object Integrity Using Rules," in Pierre America (ed.), *Lecture Notes in Computer Science, ECOOP '91, European Conference on Object-Oriented Programming,* Springer-Verlag, July 1991.
4. F. Cacace, S. Ceri, S. Crespi-Reghizzi, L. Tanca, and R. Zicari, "Integrating Object-Oriented Data Modeling with a Rule-Based Programming Paradigm," *Proceedings of the 1990 ACM SIGMOD International Conference on the Management of Data,* Atlantic City, NJ, May 1990, vol. 19, No. 2, June 1990.
5. Yves Caseau and Glenn Silverstein, "Some Original Features of the LAURE Language," position paper at OOPSLA 1992, October 1992.
6. David Hutchison and Jonathan Walpole, "Distributed Systems and Objects," in Gordon Blair, John Gallagher, David Hutchison, and Doug Shepherd (eds.), *Object-Oriented Languages, Systems and Applications,* Halsted Press, 1990.
7. R. Morrison, A. L. Brown, R. C. H. Connor, Q. I. Cutts, and G. Kirby, "Protection in Persistent Object Systems," *Security and Persistence,* Bremen 1990, Workshops in Computing, series edited by Professor C. J. van Rijsbergen, Springer-Verlag.
8. Avi Silberschatz, Michael Stonebraker, and Jeff Ullman, "Next Generation Database Systems—Achievements and Opportunities," *Communications of the ACM,* vol. 34, no. 10, October 1991, pp. 110–120.

Glossary of Terms

abstract class A class that acts as a template for other classes. It is usually used as the root of a class hierarchy.

activation Copying the persistent data and associated persistent form of methods into the executable address space to invoke the operation of methods on the data.

actor A model of concurrent computation in distributed systems. Computations are carried out in response to communications sent to the actor system.

application objects Applications and their components that are managed within an object-oriented system. Operations on such objects include open, install, move, and remove.

atomicity The property that ensures that an operation either changes the state associated with all participating objects consistent with the request, or changes none at all. If a set of operations is atomic, then multiple requests for those operations are serializable.

attribute A conceptual notion employed to express an identifiable association between the object and some other entity or entities.

behavior The observable effects of performing the requested service.

binding The process of selecting a method to perform a requested service and selecting the data to be accessed by that method.

C++ An object-oriented language based on C.

class Template from which objects can be created. It is used to specify the behavior and attributes common to all objects of the class.

class inheritance The process of defining a class in terms of some existing class, by means of incremental modification.

client object An object making a request for a service.

common facilities A component of the OMA architecture that provides facilities useful in many application domains which are made available through OMA-compliant class interfaces.

data abstraction Viewing data objects in terms of the operations with which they can be manipulated rather than as elements of a set. The representation of the data object is irrelevant.

data model   A collection of entities, operators, and consistency rules.

delegation   The situation in which each object is considered an instance without a class, and new

objects can be defined in terms of other objects. Attributes are delegated from base objects to the new objects.

differential programming   Creating a new class of objects by making small changes to an existing class.

dynamic binding   Binding that is performed at run time, after the request has been issued.

encapsulation   The facility by which access to data is restricted to legal access. Illegal access is prohibited in an object by encapsulating the data and providing the member functions as the only means of obtaining access to the stored data.

extensibility   A measure of how easily software is modified.

genericity   Technique for defining software components that have more than one interpretation depending on the parameters representing types.

hierarchy   Arrangement of the set of superclasses and subclasses derived from them in a treelike structure, with the superclasses on top of classes derived from them. Such an arrangement is called a "hierarchy of classes."

inheritance   The mechanism by which new classes are defined from existing classes. Subclasses inherit operations of their parent class. Inheritance is the mechanism by which reusability is facilitated. It is a mechanism for sharing behavior and attributes between classes. It allows one class to be defined in terms of another class. Objects can inherit data and methods from other objects. Inheritance helps implement "is-a" or "kind-of" relationships.

instance variables   Variables representing the internal state of an object.

metaobject   An object that represents a type, operation, class, method, or other object model entity that describes objects.

member functions   Functions that are used to implement different operations on the object. They are part of the specification of a class.

message   The process of invoking an operation on an object. In response to a message, the corresponding method is executed in the object. A message to an object specifies what should be done. A message can be sent by clients of the object—application programs, another object, or another method within the same object.

methods   Implementations of the operations relevant to a class of objects. The part of an object that performs an operation is termed a method. Methods are invoked in response to messages.

multiple inheritance   When a class inherits from more than one base class, this is called multiple inheritance. In most OOPLs, a subclass inherits from more than one superclass. Instances of classes with multiple inheritance have instance variables for each of the inherited superclasses.

object   A combination of data and the collection of operations that are implemented on the data; also, a collection of operations that share a state. The representation of a real-world entity. An object is used to model a person, place, thing, or event from the real world. It encapsulates data and operations that can be used to manipulate the data and responds to requests for service.

object services   A component of the OMA that provides basic functions for object life-cycle management and storage.

ObjectStore   A popular OODBMS developed by Object Design Inc. It provides the facility to store complex data. Persistence is orthogonal to type in ObjectStore.

OODB   Object-oriented database.

OODBMS   Object-oriented database management system that can be used to store and retrieve objects.

ORB   Object Request Broker, the facility that provides the means by which objects make and receive requests and responses.

persistence   The ability of data to exist beyond the scope of the program that created it. The phenomenon whereby data outlive the program execution time and exist between executions of a program. All databases support persistence. In some OODBMSs, persistence is orthogonal to type, while in others, only objects belonging to classes that are derived from the persistent class or its descendants can be persistent.

polymorphism   Ability to apply the same operation to different classes of objects. The operation on the object can be invoked without knowing its actual class.

prototype   The default behavior of a concept. Other objects which are similar to a prototype can reuse parts of the representation and features of a prototype by specifying how they differ from the prototype.

query   An activity that involves selecting objects from implicitly or explicitly identified collections based on a specified predicate.

request   An event consisting of an operation and zero or more actual parameters that causes a service to be performed.

reusability   The concept of easily using existing software within new software; the ability to use well-designed software modules that have been tested, in several places, in different applications, so as to minimize development of new code. Object-oriented languages employ inheritance as a mechanism for reusability.

self-reference   The ability of a method to determine the actual object identified in the request for the service being performed by the method.

signature   Definition of the types of the parameters for a given operation.

Smalltalk   One of the first object-oriented languages. It provides an integrated software development environment, including the facility to display multiple windows and browse through classes.

structured programming   Software development methodology which employs functional decomposition and a top-down design approach for developing modular software; traditional programming techniques of breaking a task into modular subtasks.

subclass   A class that inherits behavior and attributes from another class. The subclass exploits reusability of design and reusability of code from its superclass.

superclass   A class that serves as a base class to another class. A superclass provides behavior and attributes to classes derived from it, by the inheritance mechanism.

this pointer   A pointer to the current object in C++. Serves as a pointer to "self."

transient object   An object whose existence is limited by the lifetime of the process or thread that created it; a volatile object or temporary object.

type   A predicate defined over values that can be used in a signature to restrict a possible parameter or characterize a possible result.

Versant   A commercially available OODBMS that includes a distributed object manager and an object storage system.

Index

ABOUT THE AUTHOR

Bindu R. Rao has been a consultant with a major international consulting firm, and an entrepreneur, at various times in his career. He has played the role of an object-oriented mentor in several projects at various companies. He specializes in object-oriented technology, object-oriented databases, data warehouse designs, and client/server technologies. He is the author of *C++ and the OOP Paradigm*, published by McGraw-Hill.

He received his Masters Degree in Computer Science from the University of Tennessee at Knoxville and worked on his doctoral program at the University of Minnesota for 3 years. He is currently the owner of Integrated Solutions.